Parsons on the Plains

Parsons on the Plains

JOHN McDOUGALL

EDITED BY

THOMAS BREDIN

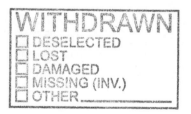

LONGMAN CANADA LIMITED

BY THE SAME AUTHOR

River of Canada
Confederation 1867
Recollections of Labrador Life (editor)
From Sea to Sea

Longman Canada Limited
55 Barber Greene Road
Don Mills, Ontario

PRINTED IN CANADA BY THE ALGER PRESS LIMITED

For Ruth

CONTENTS

1   *Parson's Son*   1

2   *From Upper Canada to Norway House*   9

3   *"Be a Man"*   17

4   *Survival Course*   27

5   *Up the Saskatchewan*   35

6   *Over the Prairie*   45

7   *Among the Plains Cree*   55

8   *First Hunt*   63

9   *Apprenticed to Rev. Woolsey*   73

10   *Winter Trips*   81

11   *The New Mission*   91

12   *Gospel Riders*   101

13   *Supporting Victoria*   113

14   *To Fort Garry*   123

15   *Waggons Home*   133

16   *Indian Friends*   147

17   *Maskepetoon: Peacemaker*   157

18   *To the Tents of the Blackfeet*   171

19   *Buffalo Pound*   179

20   *Newlywed*   191

Parsons on the Plains

ONE ≪≪

Parson's Son

My parents were pioneers. I was born on the banks of the Sydenham River in a log house, one of the first dwellings which made up the frontier village of Owen Sound. This was in the year 1842.

My earliest recollections are of stumps, log heaps, great forests, corduroy roads, Indians, log and birch-bark canoes, bateaux, Mackinaw boats. I have also a vivid recollection of deep snow in winter, and of hot weather and myriad mosquitoes in summer.

My father was first settler, trapper, trader, sailor, and local preacher, one of the grand army of pioneers who took possession of the wilderness of Ontario. Mother was a strong Christian woman — content, patient, plodding, full of quiet, restful assurance, pre-eminently qualified to be the companion and helper of one who had to hew his way in the wildness of this new world.

My mother says I spoke Indian before I spoke English. My first memories are of these original dwellers in the land. I grew up amongst them, ate corn soup out of their wooden bowls, roasted green ears at their campfires, feasted with them on deer and bear's meat, went with them to set their nets and to spear fish at nights by the light of birch-bark flambeaux or fat pine light-jack torches. Bows and arrows, paddles and canoes were my play-things, and the dusky forest children were my playmates.

Very early in my childhood, Father taught me how to swim and later on to shoot and skate and sail. Many a trip I had with my father on his trading voyages to the Manitoulin and other islands of Lake Huron and Georgian Bay. There he would obtain his loads of fish, furs, and maple sugar, and sail with these to Detroit and other eastern and southern ports.

Father had for cook and general servant a coloured man, Isaiah by name. Isaiah was my special friend; I was his particular charge. His bigness and blackness and great kindness made him a hero in my boyish mind. My contact with Isaiah and my associ-ation with the Indians very early made a real democrat of me. I never could bear to hear a black man called a "nigger" nor an Indian a "buck."

Sometimes I went with Father to his appointments to preach in the homes of the new settlers. What deep snow, what narrow roads, what great, dark, sombre woods we drove through! How solemn the meetings in those humble homes! How poor some of the people were—little clearings in the great forests; rough, unhewn logs, with trough roofs. How those people did sing! What loud amens!

Then as now the cursed liquor traffic ruined many a white man and his family. Many a poor Indian was either burned, or drowned, or killed in some way because of the trade which was carried on in this death-dealing stuff. The white man's greed, sel-fishness, and gross brutality too often found a victim in his weaker red brother. My father was a strong temperance man.

When I was between six and seven years of age, my father arranged to go to college. He left my brother David with our uncle who lived up in the bush, and me with a Mr. Cathey who taught the Mission School at Newash. Mother was quite broken up with grief at the parting from her boys, and no doubt Father felt it as keenly; but his strong will was master, and believing in Providence, he took this step, as he thought, in the path of duty and in the interest of each one of us.

My guardians were good and kind people. They believed in industry and thrift, and indeed had sore need to, for the salary of a teacher on an Indian mission in those days was very small. My time was spent in going to school, in carrying wood and water, and running errands.

Father did not remain very long at college. An opening came to him to go to Alderville and become the assistant in the management of an industrial school situated there. Father in turn opened the way for my guardian, Mr. Cathey, to become a teacher at this institution. So, we moved.

This was a great trip for me — by steamboat from Owen Sound to Coldwater, by stage to Orillia, by steamboat to Holland Landing, by stage to Toronto, and by steamboat from Toronto to Cobourg. All this was an eye and mind opener — those wonderful steamboats, the stagecoach, the multitude of people, the great city of Toronto, for even in 1850 this was to me a wonderful place.

Father's life at Alderville was a busy one: the boys to manage, and some of those grown into young men were very unruly; the farm to run, coupled with circuit and mission work. Here, a little sister was born. We named her Eliza. The Indians called her No-No-Cassa, or hummingbird, for she was a great crier.

Our stay at Alderville was not a long one. Within a year my father was commissioned by the Church to open a mission somewhere in the north country, among the needy tribes who frequented the shores of lakes Huron and Superior. He determined to locate near the confluence of the "Soo" and Garden rivers.

Behold us, then, moving out by wagon, on to Cobourg, and taking steamboat from there to Toronto; thence staging across to Holland Landing. Then going aboard the steamer *Beaver*, we landed one evening at Orillia, took stage at once, and pounded across many corduroy bridges to Coldwater, where, in the early morning, we went aboard the little side-wheeler *Gore*, and then out to Owen Sound, where my brother David joined us, and we sailed across Georgian Bay, up through the islands into the majestic river which connects these great lakes, and landed at the Indian village of Garden River.

We rented a small one-roomed house from an Indian, and into this we moved from the steamboat. Whiskey was king here. Nearly all the Indians were drunk the first night of our arrival. Such a noise and din! We children were frightened, and were very glad when morning dawned.

We went to work to build a mission house, a church, and a schoolhouse. Father was everywhere—in the bush chopping logs, among the Indians preaching the Gospel, and fighting the whiskey traffic. I drove the oxen and hauled the timber to its place. I interpreted for Father in the home and by the wayside.

My brother and I fished, picked berries, did anything to supplement our scanty fare, for Father's salary was only $320 and prices were very high. In our wanderings after berries I had to be responsible for my brother. The Indian boys would go with us. Every little while I would shout, "David, come on!" They would take it up, "Dape-tic-o-mon!" This was how the sounds came to their ears, and this they named my brother. My Indian name was "Pa-ke-noh-ka" or "the Winner." I earned this by beating all boys of my age in footraces.

After some months of hard work we got our home up, and moved into it. Then the schoolhouse was erected. A wonderful change was going on in the meantime. A strong temperance feeling took hold of the Indians. Many of them were converted. What meetings I attended with Father in the houses, and camps, and sugar-bushes of the people!

Many a long trip I had with Father in sail or Mackinaw boat, away up into Lake Superior, then down to the Bruce Mines, calling *en route* and preaching to a few Indians who lived at Punkin Point. We sailed when the wind would let us. Then Father would pull and I would steer, on into the night, across long stretches and along what seemed to me interminable shores.

How sleepy I used to be! Often I wondered if Father ever became tired. He would preach, and pray, and sing, and then pull, as if he were fresh all the time.

Then, in winter, with our little white pony and jumper, which my father had made, we would take the same trips. Sometimes the ice would be very dangerous, and Father would take the reins out of the rings and give them to me straight from the horse's mouth, saying, "If she breaks through, John, keep her head above water if you can." And then Father would take the axe he carried and run ahead, trying the ice as he ran. And thus we would reach those early settlements and Indian camps, where Father was always welcome.

In summer, in coming to or from Lake Superior, we always portaged at the "Soo," on the American side. Coming down, Father would put me ashore at the head of the rapids, and he would run them.

Some of this time Mother was very sick and David and I had all the work to do about the house — wash, scrub, bake, cook, inside and outside. We found plenty to do. When not wanted at home we went fishing and hunting. Then I found employment in teaming.

I worked one winter for an Indian, hauling saw-logs out of the woods to the river bank. He gave me fifty cents per day and my board. In the summer, I sometimes sold cordwood on commission for Mr. Church, the trader, and when he put up a sawmill, a couple of miles down the river, I several times got out a lot of saw-logs and rafted them down to the mill.

After six years of great toil, and a good deal of privation, Father was moved to Rama. Now a bright new field was opening before me, for Father had determined to send me to Victoria College. I was nearly fourteen years old. At that time there was a preparatory department in connection with the college. So, soon after we were settled at Rama, I went on to Cobourg.

I was lonesome and completely lost in those strange surroundings. It was days before I became in any way acquainted with the boys. I was pointed out by one boy to another as the "Indian fellow."

I was given a chum and he was as full of mischief and conceit as boys generally are in the presence of one not so experienced as they are. Noticing that I stuck to my Latin grammar a great deal, one day when I was out of the room, he smeared the pages of my lesson with mucilage and shut the book. Another time he knotted and twisted my Sunday clothes as they hung in the room.

Now my temper was up. I went out on to the playground, found him among a crowd, and caught him by the throat, tripped him up and got on top of him.

"Call me an Indian, eh! I'll Indian you, I'll scalp you," I said.

With one hand on his throat, I felt for my knife with the other, when he began to call "Murder!"

The other boys pulled me off, but I explained to them how he had treated me. They took my part and I was introduced. After that everybody knew me, and I had lots of friends.

Soon the busy months passed, and then convocation and holidays, and I went back to Rama and enjoyed a short holiday in canoeing down to Muskoka, having as my companions my cousin Charles and my brother David.

When we came home I engaged to work for Thomas Moffatt of Orillia for one year, for $5.00 per month and my board. My work was attending shop, and one part especially was trading with the Indians. Of these we had two classes — those who belonged to the reserve at Rama, and the pagans who roamed the "Muskoka country." Having the language and intimate acquaintance with the life and habits of these people, I had the advantage over many others.

Many a wild ride I have had with those "Muskoka fellows." If we heard of them coming, I would go to meet them with a big team and sleigh, and bring them and their furs to town, and after they had traded would take them for miles on their way. While in town we would try and keep them from whiskey, but sometimes after we got started out some sly fellow would produce his bottle, and the drinking would begin, and with it the noise and bluster. I would be very glad when I got them out of my sleigh and had put some distance between us.

I was very busy and happy during my stay in Orillia. My employer and his good wife were exceedingly kind. At the end of the year I had saved all but ten dollars of my sixty-dollar salary, and with this and my father's hearty encouragement, I started for college once more.

That year at college, 1859-60, is a green spot in my memory. It opened to me a new life; it gave me the beginnings of a grip of things; it originated, or helped to originate, within me a desire to think for myself. Everywhere—on the playground, in the classrooms, in the college halls, in the students' room—I had a good time. I was strong and healthy, and for my age a more than average athlete. I could run faster and jump farther than most of the students or town boys. I knew my parents were making sacrifices to keep me at college, and I studied hard to make the most of my grand opportunity.

Thus the months flew almost too quickly, and college closed and I went home, glad to see my mother and brothers and sisters, and to launch the canoe and fish by the hour for bass and catfish, and even occasionally a maskinonge.

In a little while my father was appointed to Norway House, Hudson Bay. This news came like a clap of thunder into our quiet home at Rama. Hudson Bay—we had a very vague idea where that was. But Norway House, who could tell us about this?

Now, it so happened that we were very fortunate, for right beside us lived Peter Jacobs. Peter had once been a missionary, and had been stationed at Norway House and Lac-la-Pluie; therefore to Peter I went for information. He told me Norway House was north of Lake Winnipeg, on one of the rivers which flow into the Nelson; that it was a large Hudson's Bay Company fort, the head post of a large district; that our mission was within two miles of the fort; that the Indians were quiet, industrious, peaceable people. "In fact," said he, "the Indians at Norway House are the best I ever saw."

In the meantime Father came home. And though I did hope to work my way through college, when my father said, "My son, I want you to go with me," that settled it. We began to make ready.

TWO «««

From Upper Canada
to Norway House

Early in July, 1860, we started on our journey. We sailed from
Collingwood on an American propeller, which brought us to
Milwaukee, on Lake Michigan. Here we took a train through a
part of Wisconsin to Lacrosse, on the Mississippi River, which
place we reached about midnight, and immediately were transferred to a big Mississippi steamer—long and broad and flat,
made to run in very shallow water.

The manner of propelling this huge craft was a very large
wheel, as wide as the boat, and fixed to the stern, and which in
its revolutions fairly churned the waters in her wake. The system
of navigation was so different: the pilot steered the boat, not by
his knowledge of the fixed channel, but by his experience of the
lights and shadows on the water which by day or night indicated
to him the deep and shallow parts.

Passengers and mails had no sooner been transferred, than
"tinkle! tinkle!" went the bells, and our big steamer quivered
from stem to stern, and then began to vibrate and shake as if in a
fit of ague, and we were out in the stream and breasting the current of this mighty river. Soon all was quiet except the noise of
the engines and the splash of the paddles.

Next day we came to Lake Pepin. Here we were joined to another big steamer. The two were fastened together side by side to run the length of the lake, and also to give the passengers of the other boat opportunity to come aboard ours and be entertained by music and dancing.

The coloured steward and waiters of our boat were a grand orchestra in themselves. One big coloured man was master of ceremonies. Above the din of machinery and splashing of huge paddles rose his voice in stentorian tones: "Right! Left! Promenade! Change partners! Swing partners!" And thus the fun went on that bright afternoon while our big stern-wheelers ploughed up the current like Siamese twins.

From port to port the pilot reigned supreme. What a lordly fellow he was! As soon as the boat was tied to the bank, the captain and mate took charge. They drove with a vengeance, putting off or taking on freight at the stopping places, and taking in cordwood from the barge towed alongside in order to save time. They made the men jump. The captain would cuff, and the mate would kick, and the two would vie with each other in profanity, and thus they rushed things. When ready, the pilot with quiet dignity would resume his throne.

When the channel narrowed our boats parted, and began a race. Throw in the pitch pine-knots! Fling in the chunks of bacon! "Make steam! More steam!" is the meaning of the ringing of bells and the messages which follow each other down from the pilot-house to the engine-room. We seemed to be about matched, when our rival pilot undertook to run between us and the bar, and in doing so ran his boat hard and fast in the sand. We gave him a parting cheer and went on, reaching St. Paul some twenty-four hours ahead.

St. Paul was then a mere village. We had reached the prairie country, woodland and plain intermixed. We did hope to catch the only steamer on the Red River of the North, but in this were disappointed. We found on inquiry that there were two means of crossing the country in sight—one by stage-coach, the other by Red River cart.

A brigade of these carts had just then come in from the north, and Father and I went out to the camp where they were. I climbed into one, but did so carefully, fearing it would collapse with my weight. All the iron on it was a thin hoop on the hub, the whole thing being bound together with rawhide. Our first sight of these Red River chariots was not favourable and made Father determine not to travel with them. We were as yet too much "tenderfeet" to risk such vehicles. Imagine Mother and my sisters jogging hundreds of miles in those springless carts!

Father then went to interview the proprietors of the stage line, and concluded a bargain with them to take us from St. Paul to Georgetown on the Red River.

Accordingly, one morning bright and early and long before breakfast, we were rolling away up the eastern bank of the Mississippi — Father, Mother and sisters inside the coach, and myself up with the driver. Our pace was good, the country we were travelling through beautiful. We stopped for the first stage at St. Anthony's Falls. Here we had our breakfast.

Our drive that day took us across the Mississippi to the village of St. Cloud, where Father, learning that the steamer on the Red River would not come up to Georgetown for some time, decided to stay over until the next coach, one week later. In the meantime we made a tent, and hunted prairie chicken, and studied German, or rather Germans, for these made up the greater part of the population.

Taking the next coach the following week, we continued our journey. Soon we left settlement behind, the people of the stagehouses and stopping places being the only inhabitants along the route. Many of these were massacred in the Sioux rising which took place shortly afterwards. Our stages ranged from twelve to twenty miles, and we averaged seventy miles per day.

My delight was to drive the four-in-hand, and the good-natured drivers gave me many an opportunity to do so. It seemed like really living to hold those reins, and swing around those hills and bowl through those valleys at a brisk trot or quick gallop.

By and by we reached the beginning of the Red River. We were across the divide; we were coursing down the country north-ward. Hitherto it had been "up north" with us, but now, for years, it would be "down north." These waters flowed down into Hudson Bay.

Presently we were on the great flat plain which largely consti-tutes the valley of the Red River. At the stopping place on the edge of this flat country, the stage people were about to leave the coach and hitch on to a broad-tired, springless wagon, but Father simply put his foot down and we went on with our coach. The stopping place was unique of its kind — a dugout with a ridge-pole and small poles leaned against this on two sides, with earth and sods placed over these poles, and some canvas hung at either end. The night was hot, the dugout, because of the cook-stove, hotter still, and the mosquitoes were there by the million. My bed was under the table on the mud floor. My companion for the night was the proprietor of this "one-roomed mud hotel."

The next morning the driver for that day said to me, "Now, young man, make a good square meal, for tonight we will reach Georgetown, and you will have only dogs and pemmican to eat." I asked him what pemmican was, but he could not tell me. All day we drove over this great flat plain of rich soil and long grass. The only break was the fringing of timber along the river. We had dinner and then supper, and again the driver admonished us to partake heartily of bacon and bread, for tonight, said he, "We reach the land of the pemmican."

Late in the evening we reached Georgetown. Here we were on the banks of the Red River, and at the end of our stage journey, where we hoped to find a steamer to take us down to Fort Garry. The town consisted of one dwelling house and a storehouse, both belonging to the Hudson's Bay Company whose posts reached far on to the Arctic and dotted the country from Labrador to the Pacific coast.

The gentleman in charge, a Mr. Murray, learning of our desti-nation, with the usual courtesy of the Hudson's Bay Company's officers welcomed us heartily. He gave up his room to our family and took up quarters with me in our tent.

That night, before we went to sleep, I inquired of Mr. Murray if he knew anything about pemmican. With a laugh he replied, "Yes, my boy, I was made acquainted with pemmican many years ago, and will be pleased to introduce you to some in the morning." I would have inquired about dogs, but my kind friend was already snoring.

I could not sleep so soon. This strange, wild, new country we had travelled through for days, these Indian, and buffalo, and frontier stories I had listened to at the stopping places, and heard from the drivers as we travelled — though I had been born on the frontier, all this was new to me. Such illimitable plains, such rich soil, such rank grass — there was a bigness about all this, and I could not help but speculate upon its future.

With the early morn we were up and, after using the Red River as our wash-dish, were soon ready to investigate our new surroundings.

The first thing was pemmican. Mr. Murray took me to the storehouse and here, sure enough, was pemmican in quantity. Cords of black and hairy bags were piled along the walls of the store. These bags were hard, and solid, and heavy. One which had been cut into was lying on the floor. Someone had taken an axe and chopped right through hair and hide and pemmican, and here it was spread before me. My friend stooped and took some and began to eat, and said to me, "Help yourself."

Though I had not eaten since supper yesterday, and we had driven a long way after that, still the dirty floor, the hairy bag, the mixture of the whole, almost turned my stomach, and I merely said, "Thank you, sir." But soon I did relish pemmican, and for years it became my staple food.

For days we waited for the steamer; not a word reached us from anywhere. In the meantime, Father and I hunted and fished. We shot duck and prairie chicken, and caught perch and pickerel and catfish and mud-turtles. And we explored the country for miles, though we were cautioned about Indians, a war party of whom one might strike anywhere and any time. By and by the steamer came, and to our great disappointment the captain said he could not run her back down as the water was too low.

The next thing was to load a flat-bottomed barge and float her down. We were allowed to erect our tent on a portion of the deck of the scow, and soon we were moving downstream, having as motive power human muscle applied to four long sweeps. Day and night, with change of men, our scow kept on down this slow-currented and tortuous stream. The only stop was to take on wood for our cooking stove. Here I learned to like pemmican.

Late in the evening of the eighth day we rounded the point at the mouth of the Assiniboine and landed at Fort Garry. It was raining hard, and mud was plentiful. I climbed the banks and saw the walls and bastions of the fort, and looked out northward on the plains and saw one house. Where that house stood, now stands the city of Winnipeg.

Fortunately for us a brigade of York boats was then loading to descend the rivers and lakes and cross the many portages to York Factory on Hudson Bay. Father lost no time in securing a passage in one of these, which was to start the next morning. In the meantime, Governor MacTavish invited Father and Mother and sisters to quarters in his own home for the night.

My work was to transfer our luggage to the York boat and then stay and look after it, for it was evident that our new crew were pretty well drunk.

Near dark we heard a strange noise up the Red, and one of the boatmen said, "Indians coming!" And sure enough a regular fleet of wild Red Lake Ojibways hove in sight and, singing and paddling in time, came ashore right beside us. They were painted and feathered, and strangely costumed. As was customary, the Hudson's Bay Company served them out a "regale" of rum, and very soon the night was made hideous with the noise of their drunken bout.

I had a big time keeping them out of our boat, but here my acquaintance with their language served me in good turn. Until near morning I kept my vigil in the bow of the boat, and then our steersman woke up, and was sufficiently sobered to relieve me. I took his blanket and slept. Our craft was an agreeable change to the clumsy barge. This was more like a bateau built and used on our eastern lakes, but lighter and stronger, capable of standing a good sea and making good time under sail. The boat was manned with eight men and a steersman. One of the eight was the bowman. Our quarters in the open boat were small and crowded.

With our eight big oars keeping stroke, we swept around the point and again took the Red for Lake Winnipeg and beyond. We had four hundred miles to make to our new home. We passed through the old Red River settlement—St. John's, St. Boniface, Kildonan, the Stone Fort and Archdeacon Cowley's Mission—then on to the mouth of the Red, where we camped at the second day.

Up to this time Father and I had not let our crew know that we understood the Ojibway or, as it was termed here, the Salteaux. Often we had been much amused at the remarks some of these men had made about us. Once, seeing a muskrat near the boat, I forgot all caution and shouted in Indian to a man with a gun to shoot it. The man let the muskrat go because of his wonder at my use of the language. *"Te wa,"* said he, "this fellow speaks as ourselves." We then became great friends.

Whenever we were wind-bound, some of the crews of the various boats would form gambling circles, and with drum and song play "odd or even," or something similar. Here the man most gifted with mind-reading power would invariably come off the winner. Our men seemed passionately fond of this form of gambling. It was one of the habits the missionary had to contend against, for often these gambling circles would break up with a stabbing or shooting scrape.

Sometimes wind-bound, sometimes sailing, sometimes pulling, presently we had gone the greater part of the length of Lake Winnipeg. We had entered one of the outward and seabound branches of the Nelson, had crossed the island-dotted Play-green lake, had come down the Jack River, and on the tenth day from Fort Garry, pulled up at Norway House.

We met a very kind welcome from the Hudson's Bay factor and his lady, and indeed from everybody. We were still two miles from Rossville. Our new friends manned a boat and took us over. Here we found the Rev. Robert Brooking and family. As no news had preceded us, we brought them word of their being relieved. Great was their joy, and ours was not a little, for here was our home.

Here were we to work and labour, each according to his ability.

THREE

"Be a Man"

Rossville is beautifully situated on a rocky promontory which stretches out into the lake. All around are coves and bays and islands and rivers. The water is living and good, the fish are of first quality, and in the season fowl of many kinds are plentiful.

Canoe and boat in summer, dog train in winter—these were the means of transport. The only horse in the country belonged to the Mission. It had been brought there by James Evans and was now very old. We used him to plough our garden and sometimes haul a little wood, but he was really a "superannuate."

The Indians were of the Cree nation and spoke a dialect of that language known as the Swampy Cree. As there is a strong affinity between the Ojibway and the Cree, I began very soon to pick it up. The occupation of these Indians was, in summer, boating for the Hudson's Bay Company and free traders, and in winter, hunting. There were no better and no hardier tripmen in the whole Hudson's Bay country than these Norway House Indians.

Between Lake Winnipeg and York Factory there are very many portages, and across these all the imports and exports for this part of the country must be carried on men's backs, and across some the big boats must be hauled. No men did the work more quickly or willingly than the men from our Mission at Rossville.

My work was teaching, and I had my hands full, for my daily average was about eighty pupils. I had no trouble to gather students during the two years I taught at Norway House. They came from the mainland and from the islands and from the fort, by canoe and by dog train. My scholars were faithful in their attendance, but the responsibility was a heavy one for me, a mere boy.

After school hours I either took my gun and went partridge hunting, or went and set my net for whitefish to help make our pot boil. On Saturdays I took one of my boys with me in my canoe, and we would paddle off to hunt ducks and other fowl.

When winter came — which it does very early there — I got some traps and set them for foxes. Many a winter morning I rose at four o'clock, harnessed my dogs, and drove miles and back in visiting my traps, reaching home and having breakfast before daylight. It was necessary for a part of the winter to begin school as soon as it was good daylight.

Soon after we arrived I invested in four pups. I paid the mission interpreter, Mr. Sinclair, two pounds sterling for them, on condition that he fed them until they were one year old. In the meantime, for the first winter, Mr. Sinclair kindly lent me some of his dogs. Everybody had dogs, and my pups promised to make a good train when they grew. All my boy pupils were great "dog-drivers."

Many a Saturday morning, bright and early, my boys would rendezvous at the mission, and we would start with staked wood-sleighs across the lake or up the river to the nearest dry wood bluff. This, in my time, was three or four miles away. What a string we would make — twenty-five or thirty boys of us, each with three or four dogs, all these hitched tandem, bells ringing, boys shouting, whips cracking, dogs yelping — away we would fly as fast as we could drive. When we reached the wood we would race to see who could chop and split and load first. What shouting and laughter and fun! And when all were loaded, back we went across the ice as fast as we could go, all running. Then we would pile our wood at the schoolhouse or church.

Agreeing to meet at the mission house in the afternoon, away home to their dinner my boys would drive, and by and by turn up, this time with flat sleds or toboggans. Now we would race across to the Hudson's Bay Company's fort, every man for himself. When we got there we would challenge the Company's employees to a game of football, for this was the national game of the Northwest, and my boys were hard to beat. Then back home by moon or Northern Light, making this ice-bound land like day. Those were great times for the cultivation of wind and muscle and speed — and better, sympathy and trust.

Father, when home, held an English service at the fort once a week, and the largest room available was always full. Then we organized a literary society which met weekly at the fort. Thus many a night we drove to and fro with our quick-moving dogs.

At times we were surrounded by the "Aurora." Sometimes they seemed to touch us. One could hear the swish of the quick movement through the crisp, frosty atmosphere. Halos of many-coloured light would envelop us. Forest and rock, ice and snow would become radiant as with heavenly glory. No wonder the Indian calls these wonderful phenomena "The Dancers," and says they are the spirits of the departed.

During our first winter I accompanied Father on a trip to Jackson's Bay and Oxford House. This is about 180 miles almost due north of Norway House, making a trip of 360 miles.

Our manner of starting out on the trip was as follows: William Rundle, father's hired man, went ahead on snowshoes, for there was no track; then came John Sinclair, the interpreter, with his dogs hitched to a cariole, which is a toboggan with parchment sides and partly covered in, in which father rode, and on the tail of which some of the necessary outfit was tightly lashed; then came my train of dogs and sleigh, on which was lashed the load, consisting of fish for dogs and pemmican and food for men, kettles, axe, bedding — in short, everything for the trip; then myself on snowshoes, bringing up the rear.

This was my first real winter trip with dogs, and I very soon found it to be desperately hard work. The driver of a dog-sleigh must do all the holding back going downhill; must right the sleigh when it upsets; keep it from upsetting along sidehills, and often push up hills; and, besides all this, urge and drive the dogs, and do all he can to make good time.

Many a time that first day I wished myself back at the Mission. The hauling of wood, the racing across to .the fort — all that had been as child's play. This was earnest work, and tough at that. The big load would cause my sleigh to upset. My snowshoes would cause me to upset. The dogs began to think — indeed, soon knew — I was a tenderfoot. They played with me.

Ahead was William Rundle, making a beeline for the north, and stepping as if he were going to reach the pole. Mr. Sinclair was close behind him, and I was far, far behind. Both spirit and flesh began to weaken. Then we stopped on an island and made a fire; that is, Father and the men had the fire about made when I came up. Father looked mischievous. I had bothered him to let me go on this trip. However, the tea and pemmican made me feel better for a while.

Away we went for the second spell, between islands, across portages, down forest-fringed rivers and bluffs casting sombre shadows. On my companions seemed to fly, while I dragged behind. Oh, how heavy those snowshoes! Oh, how lazy those dogs! Oh, how often that old sleigh upset! I was almost in a frenzy with mortification at my failure to be what I had presumed to think I was.

When are they going to camp? Why don't they camp? These were questions I kept repeating to myself. We were going down a river. It was now late. I would expect to find them camped around the next point. Alas! Yonder they were disappearing around another point. Often I wished I had not come, and dragged wearily on, legs aching, back aching, almost soul aching.

Finally they did camp. I came up at last and heard the axes ringing. They had climbed the bank and gone into the forest. I pushed my sleigh up and unharnessed my dogs. I had just got the collar off the last one in time to hear Father say, "Hurry, John, and carry up the wood." I felt more like having someone carry me.

Carrying ten- and twelve-foot logs on snowshoes is no fun. By great dint of effort you get the log on to your shoulder and then step out. Deep and loose snow, bushes and the limbs of trees, and your own legs and arms conspire to trip and bother. Many a fall is inevitable. And there are a great many logs to be carried, for the nights are long and cold. William felled the trees and cut them into lengths, and I grunted and grumbled under their weight to the pile beside the camp.

In the meanwhile Father and his interpreter were making camp, which was no small job. First they went to work, each with a snowshoe as a shovel to clear the snow away for a space about twelve feet square, down to the ground or moss. Thus snow formed the walls of our camp. These walls were then lined with pine boughs, and the bottom was floored with the same material. Then the fire was made on the side away from the wind. It occupied the whole length of one side.

Except in the case of a snowstorm, there would be no covering overhead. If the snow was falling thick, some small poles would be stuck in the snowbank at the back of the camp, with a covering of canvas or blankets as a temporary roof.

At last we were done. The camp was made, the wood was carried, and the fire was blazing.

Then the sleighs must be untied and what you wanted for that time taken from them. Then carefully you must rewrap and retie your sleigh. Sometimes you must even make a staging on which to hang it to keep it and its contents from your dogs. Many a time when provisions were short, and our dogs were very hungry, I have had to hang up not only all eatables, but the sleighs and harness also, for these were largely bound and made of leather and rawhide, and the hungry dogs would eat all of this if they had the chance.

Now comes supper, and while this is cooking we stand our frozen whitefish around the fire in order to thaw them before we feed them to the dogs. These we feed at night only. The poor fellows must go the twenty-four hours on one meal. The ration at this time is six whitefish to each train of four dogs. Each driver takes his dogs apart and stands whip in hand to prevent them robbing one another.

After supper, those who smoke light their pipes, and we dry our moccasins and duffels if these need it. Then accounts of old trips and camp storms are in vogue. Our fire is a big one, but our room is a big one also, being all out of doors. While your faces and fronts are burning, your back is freezing, and you turn around every little while to equalize things. While all this is going on, my legs, unused to the snowshoes' strain and the long tramp, are every little while causing me great pain by taking cramps. I do not say anything about this, but I think a lot. I know Father understands the case, but except for a twinkle of his eye he gives no sign that he thinks of it.

Presently we make up our beds, and sing a hymn, and have prayer. We lie down as we travelled, except our belts — coats and caps all on — and in order to keep warm, we should lie perfectly still. The least move will let the cold in. But how was I to remain still when my legs refused to remain quiet? Every little while a cramp would take hold and the pain would be dreadful, but with desperation I would strive to keep still, for I was sleeping with Father. I could not sleep, and when my legs ceased to pain, and I was about to fall asleep, Father lit a match, looked at his watch, and said, "Hurrah, boys, it is time to get up."

It was now about three o'clock, and we made a slight breakfast on pemmican and tea, had a short prayer, and tied on our bedding and camp outfit, and harnessed our dogs. Mind you, this lashing and tying of sleds and catching and harnessing of dogs was hard on the fingers, and often very trying to the temper, for those cunning dogs would hide away in the bush, and sometimes we had to catch and tie the worst ones up before we made any move towards a start, or else they would run away.

It was now about four o'clock or a little after, and we retraced our track to the river and again turned our faces northward. My companions seemed to leave me almost at once. The narrow winding river, with its forest-clad banks, was dark and very cold and dreary. My legs were stiff, and my feet were already sore with the snowshoe strings. My dogs were indifferent to my urging. They knew I would not run out of the trail to get at them with my whip. Many a time that cold, dark, winter's morning I wished I was at home or in Ontario.

I became sleepy. Even my slow-going dogs would leave me, and I would make a desperate effort to come up again, and thus the hours passed and we kept to the river. After a long time, a terrible time to me, the day sky began to appear. Slowly the morning dawned, and the cold intensified. I was in misery. I began to wonder where my friends would stop for breakfast.

Presently we came to a large lake. Out a mile or two I could discern an island. That, I thought, is where they will stop. They were near it already, and I began to hope for rest. Again I looked, and straight past it William took his course, and away yonder, like a faint streak of blue, was a point he was making for. It seemed I would have to give up.

I was now a considerable distance behind my dogs when all of a sudden a feeling took hold of me, and I began to reason with myself. What is the matter with you? What are you doing behind here, ready to give up? You are strong and capable. Come on! Be a man! I stepped out briskly and I began to run on those snowshoes. I came up to those lazy dogs and gave them such a shout they thought a small cyclone had struck them. Soon I was up opposite the island, and I ran away to its shore, broke a long dry pole, and after my dogs I went. I brought it down alongside them with another shout, and made them bound off. Then picking up the pieces of broken pole, I let them fly at those dogs, and away we went.

Presently I was in a glow, and the stiffness in my limbs was gone, and soon I came up to my companions, and said, "Where are you going to have breakfast?" And they said, "Across yonder," pointing to the blue streak in the distance. "Well, then," said I, "why don't you travel faster, and let us get there?"

William looked at me. Father turned round in his cariole to see if I was in earnest. From then on I was all right. No more whining and dragging behind after that. When we stopped for breakfast, father smiled at me in a new way. I had come up in his estimation. I overhead William say to Mr. Sinclair, "John is all right, he has found his legs."

Across the lake, over the portages, through the forests, up and down rivers, steadily we kept on our course. At one of our encampments we made a cache of some fish and some pemmican for our return journey. The manner of our doing so was to rake away the embers and coals from where we had the fire during the night and morning, and then dig a hole in the thawed ground, and put our provisions in this hole; then cover it with a few sticks; and put the earth back, until the place was full; then make a small fire just over the spot, and in going away kick some snow into the fireplace. This would soon freeze hard, and the ashes and embers would destroy the scent, and thus the cunning wolverine would not find our cache.

At the southerly end of Oxford Lake we found a single camp of Indians, and stopped with them for the night. They feasted us on young beaver, which was an agreeable change from pemmican. There were seventeen of us in that camp for the night. It was circular, and may have been twelve feet in diameter. On the ground we lay with our feet to the fire. During the night I felt my foot very hot, and springing up, found that my part of the blanket was burned through and my duffel sock was on fire. This was another tenderfoot experience.

The next day we reached Jackson's Bay, where we received from Mr. and Mrs. Stringfellow, the missionary and his wife, a very hearty welcome. We spent Saturday and part of Sunday here. Mr. Stringfellow went with us to the fort, and Father held a service in the evening. His address, which was in English, Mr. Sinclair afterwards gave almost verbatim to those who understood only Cree, which seemed to me a remarkable feat of memory, seeing he had not taken other than mental notes.

We returned on Monday to Jackson's Bay, and left on Tuesday

for Norway House and found our cache all right. We reached home on Friday afternoon, averaging forty-five miles per day, which, considering there had been a good deal of storm and our outward track in many places could not be seen, was very fair time.

FOUR

Survival Course

Some time after getting back to Rossville, my father determined to enlarge the church. The Hudson's Bay Company offered to send their carpenters to do the work, if the missionary and Indians got out the timber and lumber. The Indians went into this work heartily. The first thing was to chop and hew the timber and saw-logs, and haul all these to some lake or river, from which it might be rafted to the mission.

Good timber was found on an island in Play-green Lake, about twenty miles away. To this place we went by dog train and on snowshoes, Father and the men chopping and hewing the timber, and myself and my schoolboys hauling it out to the shore and piling it ready for rafting in the summer. My boys and I had the roads to make as well.

Our open camp was a unique sight in the evening. Big fires stretched along the centre, a brush floor down both sides. There was fish thawing, fish boiling, fish roasting, fish frying. Our pemmican we saved for breakfast, as it did not require time to cook; then fish is more digestible, therefore better for supper. Men and boys were sitting and standing, some cooking, some mending moccasins, others drying them — all good-natured and happy. Behind all this, but still in the light of the fire, were the dogs. They were of all breeds and of all colours, some lounging, some snarling, some fighting — all waiting for their supper, which was thawing at the fire.

After supper the dogs were fed, and then the woods would echo with hearty singing. Father was a good singer, and between us we taught these people many new songs and hymns.

A few weeks later there was great excitement in the village. The first goose of the season had been seen. To men who have been living for the most part on fish during the winter months, the coming of the geese from the south is a welcome change. Presently from all over the village the boys were imitating the wild goose's call, and the old hunters were getting their decoy heads ready. As for the bodies, they could make them out of logs near or at the place they might select for a hunting ground.

Father and I went several times to places nearby. I had a single-barrelled muzzle-loading gun. We would go Friday evening and come home Saturday evening. Father was an ardent sportsman and a good shot. The Hudson's Bay factor and clerks went a long distance and were away some weeks on the goose hunt.

About the last of May, when the ice went off the lake and the navigation was open, we made up another bee to go to raft our timber down. Father sent William and me one day ahead of the party in order that we might set nets for sturgeon. When they came up next day, we had fourteen. While whitefish is the staple food in that north country, sturgeon come in at seasons as an extra luxury. Indeed, they are the beef and bacon of the northern Indian. Sturgeon oil is both lard and butter for these people, and blessed is the wife and mother who has many vessels full of it.

We made a big raft of our timber, and both wind and current favouring us, we soon had it hauled out and piled up on the beach near the church. The sawing of the timber was done by the Indians in turn, each doing his share. This we carefully piled to season, and in the autumn the Hudson's Bay Company, as per offer and promise, sent their carpenters and the enlargement went on. There was great rejoicing and a grand reopening when the work was finished.

Now Norway House was the first depot post in the interior, coming from York Factory on the Hudson's Bay. Here were wintered the most of the "green hands," those men who had been brought out by the ship the previous summer, and from this point these men were distributed to the various districts in the farther interior. As the summer months are few in that northern climate, the need to push transport is imperative.

To Norway House, in the early summer, came the brigade of boats from the Mackenzie River, the Athabasca, and English River, and Cumberland districts. Down from the west, the Saskatchewan and Swan River districts, came the "Braroes" (I give the word as it was pronounced), the men from the great plains. Down from the south, the Red River Brigade added their quota to these fleets of inland transport.

For all these Norway House was the common centre. At those times the old fort was *en fête*. The river banks were lined far up and down with boats and tents. The smoke of many camp-fires hung over the place. The prattle of many tongues in different languages was heard. English and French, and Norwegian and Ojibway, or Salteaux, and Chippewayan, and Caughnawaga and Cree were most common at these gatherings, but through and over all the Cree dominated and was most generally understood and spoken.

Here were the Governor and chief factors and chief traders and clerks of various grades in the service of this honourable Company. Here were the steersmen and bowsmen and middlemen, the hardy *voyageurs* whose strength of brain and muscle, and whose wonderful pluck and daring, as well as prudence, made possible the import and export traffic in vast regions which would have seemed to other men impossible and inaccessible. Some of these men would leave their distant inland posts on snowshoes, and reaching what was the frontier post to them in their sublime isolation, would take to the boats with first break of navigation. Then, descending rivers and running rapids and portaging falls, they would finally reach York Factory, where after unloading and reloading they would turn and retrace their course, and only arrive at their own district by the beginning of winter. Then with snowshoes and dog trains they would travel to their own homes. The toil and hardship of such a life is beyond the conception of most minds.

These gatherings were periods of great responsibilities and also of intense anxiety to the missionary stationed at Norway House. These were the days of temptation to the people. Rum and evil association were rife during this time. Then there came within the range of the missionary's influence men who had seldom been at service and many who had not had the opportunity of attending a regular preaching service for a long time. To say the right word to those who in a few days would scatter, who in a few weeks would be located at widely distant posts, but who now gathered in the mission church and eagerly listened to the preached Gospel — truly this was a great responsibility for the missionary.

The men of our mission would now be starting with their brigade of boats for the summer's transport work. To counsel with these, to arrange the work of the class-reader and local preacher, to re-admonish as to Sabbath observance and general deportment — all this kept the missionary busy and anxious.

Father was active in season and out of it. Both among Indians and white men, his influence was very apparent and became widespread in its effect for good.

In the autumn of 1861, Father and Mr. Sinclair and William made a canoe trip to Oxford House. On the return journey their canoe upset in a rapid. It was in the early morning, and Father had his heavy coat on and was otherwise handicapped for such an event. But faithful William swam to the overturned canoe, and then pushed it, end on, to Father, at the same time saying, "Keep up, master. I am coming!" And when near with the canoe, "Now, master, take hold. Hold hard!" Thus these two passed through the rapid and, swinging into an eddy at its foot, were saved. Mr. Sinclair swam ashore at once, being in light working costume.

That same fall, William was bitten on the tip of the finger by a jackfish he was taking out of the net. Inflammation set in the wound, and though Father and Mother did all they could to help him, mortification followed and he died. Night and day Father was with the poor fellow, and we all mourned for him, for his was a noble heart and he was one of God's heroes.

At the beginning of the fall fishing, as the Indians were scattered for miles in every direction and my school was broken up, my father sent me to establish a fishery. So, with a young Indian companion I went into camp across the lake, and we got to work setting our nets and making our stagings, as all fish caught before freeze-up are hung from stagings.

First, you put up good stout posts on which you lay logs, and across these you place strong poles about two and a half feet apart. Then, you cut good straight willows about an inch in thickness and three feet long. You sharpen one end of these and, punching a hole in the tail of the fish, you string the fish on the willows, ten to a stick. With a forked pole you lift these to the staging, hanging them across between the poles. There they hang, and dry, and freeze, until you haul them away to your storehouse. After ice makes, the fish freeze almost as soon as you take them out of the water, and are piled away without hanging.

When the fish are plentiful, you visit your nets two and three times in the night in order to relieve them of the great weight and strain of so many fish. In taking whitefish out of the net, one uses teeth and hands. You catch the fish in your hand, lift it to your mouth, and, taking hold of its head with your teeth, you press down its length with both hands meeting, and thus force the fish from the net without straining your net. When the fish is loose from the net, you give a swing with your head, and thus toss the fish into the boat behind you or away out on the ice beside you.

When the lakes and rivers are frozen over, you take a long rope, about a quarter of an inch in thickness, and pass it under the ice to the length of your net. To do this you take a long dry pole and fasten your rope at one end of it. Then you cut holes in the ice the length of your pole apart. This is done in the direction you want to set your net. Now you pass the pole under the ice, using a forked stick to push it along, and in this way bring your line out at the far end of where your net will be when set. One pulls the rope and the other sets the net, carefully letting floats and stones go as these should in order that the net hang right.

Overhauling the nets, taking care of the fish, mending and drying the nets keeps you busy almost all the time. And all of this, except mending the nets in the tent, is desperately cold work. The ice forms on your sleeves and clothing. Your hands would freeze were it not that you keep them in the water as much as possible.

In my time hundreds of thousands of whitefish were thus taken every year for winter use, the principal food for men and dogs being fish. My companion and I put up about two thousand whitefish, besides a number of jackfish. These were hauled home by dog train.

My four pups which I bought from Mr. Sinclair over a year since were now fine big dogs, but as wild as wolves. I had put up a square of logs for a doghouse, and by feeding, and coaxing, and decoying with old dogs, I finally succeeded in getting them into it. Then I would catch one at a time and hitch him with some old and trained dogs. Father would go with me and fight off the other three while I secured the one I was breaking in. By and by I had the whole four broken, and they turned out splendid fellows to pull and go. Very few, if any, trains could leave me in the race. When I loaded them with two hundred hung fish, they would keep me on the dead run to follow.

I was very proud of my first train of dogs and of my success in breaking them. Many a flying trip I gave Father or Mother and my sisters over to the fort or out among the Indians. Sometimes I went with Father to visit Indian camps, and also to the Hudson's Bay shanties away up Jack River where their men were taking out timber and wood for the fort. Father was well wrapped in the cariole and I, having to run and keep the swinging cariole right side up, had not time to get cold.

During this second winter Father sent me down to Oxford House. I had quite a load for the Rev. Mr. Stringfellow. One item was several cakes of frozen cream which mother sent to Mrs. Stringfellow. We had a cow; they had none. We happened to strike the very coldest part of the winter for the trip. There were four of us in the party — two Indians returning to Jackson's Bay, my companion and myself. When we reached the Bay, my companions were spotted with frost-bites — great black scars on the forehead and cheeks and chin.

When we reached Mr. Stringfellow's in the morning, the thermometer registered 56° below zero. We had camped the night before on an island in Oxford Lake, and started out at three o'clock, and one can imagine what it must have been about daylight that morning with heavy snowshoeing. On the way back, my young Indian and I made the return trip in three days, averaging sixty miles per day.

All of this fishing and dog-driving and travelling was just so much practice and experience for the years to come in farther and far more difficult fields. I did not know this at the time, but so it turned out.

FIVE

Up the Saskatchewan

As the missions on the Saskatchewan were under Father's chairmanship, he decided to visit them during the summer of 1862 and to take me along. At the invitation of the Hudson's Bay officers, he went with them to Red River and then rode on horseback across the plains to Fort Carlton on the Saskatchewan. He arranged for me to go to the same point by boat.

Our route was up the Jack River, across the Play-green Lake to Lake Winnipeg, and then across its northern end. Favouring winds and fine weather brought us to the mouth of the Saskatchewan in two or three days.

Here are the Grand Rapids. They are about three miles long. Up the first two miles the boats are pulled and poled and tracked. Then comes the tug-of-war. Everything must be taken out of the boat and carried across the portage. Then the pulling of the boats across comes next. This is done on skids and rollers, and all by man's strength alone. The ordinary load that a man carries over the portage is two pieces, averaging one hundred pounds each. The man carries one piece on his back, sustained by a strap on his forehead; then upon this the other piece is placed. This leans up against his neck and head and acts as a brace. Away trots the man. Mosquitoes and mud, valley and hills, he must "get there." The whole matter was slavish and, in the long run, costly.

The second day, in the evening, we were across the portage and loaded up, all ready for a new start, which we made early next morning. The current was rapid. Now poling, now pulling, then with a line out tracking, slowly we worked up the big Saskatchewan. Crossing Cedar Lake, we entered the steady current of this mighty river.

Here we were overhauled one evening by a couple of big inland canoes manned by Iroquois Indians, conveying Governor Dallas, who had succeeded Sir George Simpson as Governor of the Hudson's Bay Company and who was now, in company with Chief Factor William Christie as escort, on his way to visit the posts of the Company in the far north and west. With grace and speed and regular dip of paddles, keeping time to their canoe song, they hove in sight and came to land beside us, and we camped together for the night.

Up and away they went early next morning to ascend the tributaries of the Saskatchewan which flow from the north country; then to make the "long portage," which would bring them to the headwaters of the great Mackenzie system; then up the Peace to the foot of the mountains, thence to return by the same route. Meanwhile the dignitaries they had conveyed thus far would now turn southwards across long stretches of woodland prairie, and on horseback and with pack-saddles, would again come out on the Saskatchewan at Edmonton.

For days our progress was very slow. Our men had to ply their oars incessantly. Many times in one day we crossed and recrossed the river to take advantage of the weaker currents. From the break of day until the stars began to twinkle at night, only stopping for meals, our men kept at it, as if they were machines and not flesh and blood. Who can describe the sweltering heat and the numberless mosquitoes they endured?

By and by we came to where there was a beach along the shore, and then our men gladly took to tracking instead of the oar. Four men would hitch themselves with their carrying-straps to the end of a long rope, and walk and run along the shore for miles, thus pulling their boat up the stream at a rapid rate. Then the other four would take the collars and our progress became faster. Sometimes we came to extra currents or rapids; then the rope was doubled, and all hands went on shore to pull and strain past the difficulty. Occasionally two crews had to come to each other's help, and take one boat at a time up the rapids, and though our men welcomed this as compared with the monotonous pull, pull, pull at the oars, it was still very hard work.

Along miles of rocky beach, then up and over steep-cut banks, now ankle or knee-deep in mud and quicksands, then up to the armpits in crossing snags and channels and mouths of tributary streams; then, "All aboard," and once more bend to the oars, to cross over to better tracking on the other side of the river; thus in constant hardship did our faithful crews slowly work their way up this mighty river.

We now caught glimpses of prairie every little while. The country was changing, the banks were becoming higher, the soil richer. We were on the divide between the swampy and rocky regions of the east and north, and the rich pastures and agricultural lands of the Saskatchewan Valley. Several times as the boats were being tracked up the river, I jumped ashore and ran across land, and was delighted to breathe the air of the plains, and scent the aroma of the wild roses, and behold for myself the rich grass and richer soils of this wonderland.

We passed Fort la Corne, and later on the mouth of the south branch. I remember distinctly climbing the bank near where the town of Prince Albert is now situated. Then it was without a single settler, but the whole land seemed to me as speaking out in strong invitation to someone to come and occupy.

Near Fort Carlton we met a fresh volume of water. Suddenly the river rose, the current strengthened, and the work became harder. The summer heat had loosened the ice and snow in the distant mountains. Fortunately for us we were near our objective when this heavy current met us, and presently the bows of our boats were hugging the bank at the landing place.

Fort Carlton I found to consist of some dwellings and stores, crowded together and surrounded by a high palisade, with bastions at its four corners, and built on a low bench on the south side of the river. A few buffalo skin lodges told me I was now in the famous buffalo country.

On going ashore I was told to run up to the fort, as dinner was now on. Finding the dining room, I sat down at the only vacant place and was asked by the gentleman at the head of the table if I would have some buffalo steak. I assented gladly. I had eaten pemmican and dried meat, but this was my first steak and I relished it very much. Presently my host asked me to have some more, but I thought I had eaten enough meat, and inadvertently I said to my nearest neighbour, "Will you please pass the bread." This produced a laugh all around the table, and an old gentleman said to me, "Young man, you are out of the latitude of bread." And so it was, for looking down the table, I saw there was no bread, no vegetables, only buffalo steak. I determined to be wiser next time.

My surroundings were now entirely different from anything heretofore in my life. The country was different, the food was different, and the Indians were distinctly different from all I had previously met. Their costume, or rather lack of any often, their highly painted faces and feathered and gew-gaw bedecked heads, their long plaits or loosely flowing hair, their gaudy blankets or fantastically painted buffalo robes, their ponies and saddles and buffalo hide and hair lines, their sinew-mounted and snakeskin-covered bows and shod arrows, their lodges and travois, both for horses and dogs—all these things were new to me.

This was a big grass country. Horses and ponies were at a premium here. The gentlemen of the Hudson's Bay Company were exceedingly kind to me. Mr. P. Tait, who was in charge of the fort, lent me horses, and I took glorious rides out on the prairie. I will never forget those first gallops on the plains. I felt

Paul Kane

Scalp Dance

Royal Ontario Museum, Toronto

even then how easy it would be for me to cast in my lot with such a life in such a land as this.

Some of us arranged a party to go and meet those we expected to be now nearby on the long trail from Red River to this point. Some Hudson's Bay clerks and myself formed the party. Several horses had been driven into the yard, and when I got there all were taken but one, which seemed to me unfit to ride any distance. Just then Mr. Tait came along and whispered, "Take him, and when you reach the horse guard, who is not far from here on your road, tell him to catch my horse Badger for you." I thanked him and saddled the old plug, and off we rode.

Many a joke I took because of my sorry steed; but I could very well stand it all, for I had quietly asked the Indian boy if he knew the horse "Badger," and his eyes glistened as he said, "I think I do; he is one of the best saddle horses around here." So I was patiently waiting my turn; and it came, for we soon reached the horse guard, and I told him what Mr. Tait had said. He took his lariat and went and caught a beautiful bay, fat and slick, and handsome as a picture. I saddled him and came up to my companions on the jump, and astonished them with the magnificence of my mount.

Now I was the envied of the party, and proud I was as my horse frisked and jumped and played under me. We galloped past Duck Lake, which long years after became the scene of the first actual outbreak in the rebellion in 1885. We rode down to the north bank of the South Saskatchewan, and camped there without bedding; and waiting part of the next day, finally turned back without any sign of our friends, and went into a grand duck hunt on the way back to Carlton, which we reached late in the evening.

At this time the old fort and the plain around was a busy scene — our crews from the boats, hunters from the plains, parties of Indians in to trade, the air full of stories about the southern Indians and the tribal wars to and fro, scalps taken and horses stolen, the herds of buffalo said to be within a hundred miles from the fort, or less than two days out. Buffalo-skin lodges and canvas tents dotted the plain in every direction. Horse races and foot races were common occurrences. I championed older Canada against Indians, half-breeds, and Hudson's Bay officials and employees, and in the foot racing and jumping — high, long, and hop, step, and jump — "cleaned out the crowd" and made a name for myself and country.

Amid such doings, Father and his party came up. Father told me that the first two days in the saddle had been trying times with him. The everlasting jog of the all-day journey made him feel so stiff and sore the first night that he was hardly able to mount his horse the next day. But after three or four days this wore off.

Mr. Hardisty, the Hudson's Bay officer who had brought Father across the plains thus far, soon made arrangements for our continuing our journey westward. He furnished us with horses and saddles and a tent, and also a man as a guide. Swimming our horses across the North Saskatchewan opposite the fort, and crossing ourselves and saddles in a boat, we saddled up and packed our one pack-horse and set out by the big hill, ascending it with more ease than the American I once met at the top of it who said to me, "That is the mostest biliousest hill I ever did climb."

We were now on the north side of the North Saskatchewan, and away we went at the orthodox jog-trot for Fort Pitt, the next post in the chain established by the Hudson's Bay Company.

Our guide was an old man with the name of La Gress, or as the Indians called him, "Grease." Mr. Hardisty had said of him, "He is a good traveller and a quick cook," all of which we found to be true. He was small and wiry, and sat his horse as if he had grown there. When on the jog his little legs incessantly moved, and his pipe seemed to everlastingly smoke. He had been to Red River and had crossed the mountains several times, had been on the plains and in the north, had been chased many a time by the enemy, had starved and almost perished once for the lack of food on one of his trips.

He was the man of whom it is told that as he sat picking the bones of a raven, he vehemently maintained to his partner that "this was a clean bird." Indeed our guide was a man full of adventure and travel. To me he was full of interest, and I plied him with questions as we jogged side by side through the country.

We rode through the Thickwood Hills. We skirted the Bear's-paddling Lake. We passed the springs into which tradition said the buffalo disappeared and emerged from occasionally. Trotting by Jack-fish Lake, on for miles through most magnificent land and grass and wood and water, we crossed the valley of the Turtle River. We rode at the foot of Red Deer Hill and French-man's Butte.

We picked up Peter Erasmus, who was associated with the Rev. Henry Steinhauer, and was now freighting for the latter from Red River to Whitefish Lake. Peter was an "A 1" interpreter, and Father hired him as a guide and interpreter for the rest of our journey. We ate up all the rations, consisting of a ham of buffalo meat and a chunk of hard grease. This we accomplished the last day at noon, and we rode into Fort Pitt the evening of the fourth day from Carlton, having averaged about fifty miles per day, which was not so bad for men new to the saddle.

Fort Pitt we found on the north bank of the Saskatchewan, standing on a commanding bench near the river, and having a magnificent outlook—a wide, long valley, enclosed by high hills, which rose terrace beyond terrace in the distance, and the swiftly flowing river coming and going with majestic bends at its feet. This was then the buffalo fort of the Saskatchewan District, the great herds coming closer and oftener to this point than to any other of the Hudson's Bay posts. This was also a famous horse-breeding spot, the grasses in the vicinity being especially adapted for that business.

Here was a hunter's paradise—plenty of buffalo and fine horses. From here went out the party and the Indian to whom the Hudson's Bay officer gave seventeen arrows, saying, "Now, let us see what you can do." The Indian modestly answered, "I can but try," and killed sixteen buffalo.

We remained over Sunday at the fort and Father held service. Monday morning saw us away, mounted on fresh horses which had been provided by the gentlemen in charge of the fort.

SIX

Over the Prairie

Our course was now more northerly. Away to the south and west, we caught glimpses of the winding valley of the big river. Around us were lakes with lawn-like banks; gems of prairie with clumps of spruce and poplar intersected by birch and willow; great hills, and broad valleys, and gently rippling streams; a cloudless sky; an atmosphere surcharged with ozone above us; good horses under us; Father and guide and myself all thoroughly optimistic in thought and outlook. We were travelling steadily and fast. We amused ourselves by locating farms and homesteads, and villages and centres of population, and running imaginary railroads through the country as we trotted and cantered from early morn until night, through those lovely never-to-be-forgotten August days of 1862.

For food we had pemmican and dried meat. Occasionally we shot chickens or ducks, but the distance we had to travel and the limited time Father had at his command forbade our doing much shooting while pemmican or dried meat lasted.

We rode over the Two Hills; we galloped along the sandy beach of Sandy Lake; we saw Frog Lake away to the right; a few miles farther on we crossed Frog Creek, then Moose Creek, then the

Dog Rump. Here I missed my first bear. He was down in a deep ravine, almost under me, and as is usual with a tenderfoot at such a time, I shot over him. Since my gun was a single-barrelled muzzle-loader, the bear had plenty of time to disappear into the thick brush down the ravine, and we had no time to follow him. On we went — over hills and across broad plains thickly swarded with peavine and rich grasses. We passed Egg Lake to the left.

Early the third day we came to Saddle Lake. On its north side we found a camp of Cree Indians. Some of these belonged to Whitefish Lake and were nominally Christians. Others were wood and plain Indians, still pagan, and without any settled home, but all glad to see us. Most of the leading men and hunters had gone across the river and out on to the plains for a hunt. We learned that Mr. Steinhauer planned a trip out to the plains for provisions, but was waiting for the report of the hunters. Father decided to hurry on to Whitefish Lake and catch Mr. Steinhauer at home.

We headed almost northeast and entered the fringe of the forest lands of the north country. We were going farther out of the course of the warpaths of the plains Indians. A plains Indian dreads a forest, does not feel at home in it, and this was the reason for the selection of Whitefish Lake as a mission centre. It was a place away from the prevailing unrest on the plains south of the Saskatchewan. Incessant watchfulness might be largely laid aside. Into this thickening forest land we trotted, a narrow bridle-path our road. Water and mud became abundant.

Within a few miles of the mission we came to the thickly wooded banks of a stream where we had to swim our horses. Here we met some Indians who were starting out on a moose hunt and to my astonishment one of them seemed to be speaking English — at least I thought so. He was shouting *"Dam, dam!"* But like all men who presume on a too-hasty judgement, I was mistaken; for the old fellow was only calling to his horse, "Tom, Tom," urging him to swim across the stream. With his accent, "t" was "d."

Resaddling and galloping on, early in the afternoon we came to the mission and found Mr. Steinhauer and family well. But, as with everybody in the West in those days, their storehouse and market was the buffalo. Since pemmican, dried meat, fish, or any kind of provision was at a premium when we arrived at Whitefish Lake, both residents and visitors had to move somewhere very soon.

Mr. Steinhauer had built a mission house and schoolhouse, and also assisted quite a number of Indians to build comfortable houses. Quite a settlement had sprung up. Of course, the bulk of all effort had rested on the missionary, but he proved equal to his work. Preacher, judge, doctor, carpenter, sawyer, timberman, fisherman, hunter, and a great traveller in that country of long distances, Mr. Steinhauer had his time fully occupied.

Soon after our arrival, a few of the Indians whose families we had passed at Saddle Lake came in. They had returned from their hunt and had been successful, and brought Mr. Steinhauer some of the meat. They had been attacked by a crowd of Indians who turned out to be friends from Maskepetoon's camp. Thus they brought us word of the whereabouts of that chief and his people, the plains Cree, whom Father was most anxious to see before he returned to Norway House.

Accordingly it was arranged that we should meet some fifteen or twenty days later on the plains "somewhere." This was very indefinite, but as near as we could plan under the conditions of the time. Mr. Steinhauer would go with his people, join those at Saddle Lake, and cross the Saskatchewan to the plains and buffalo. We would go to Smoking Lake, find Mr. Woolsey, and then strike out also for the plains and the buffalo. There we hoped to meet in a large gathering before long.

We left Whitefish Lake Friday evening, having with us for the first few miles Ka-Kake or "the Hawk" and some of his people who were returning to Saddle Lake. Ka-Kake was far more than an ordinary personality. His very appearance denoted this. The elasticity of his step, the flash of his eye, the ring of his voice — you *had* to notice him. To me he was a new type. He filled my ideal as a hunter and warrior.

From Peter I learned that he was brave and kind, and full of resource, tact, strategy, and pluck. These were the striking traits of this man, by whose side I loved to ride, and later on, in whose skin-lodge I delighted to camp. He had figured in many battles and been the chief actor in many hunting fields. He had surpassed other famous buffalo hunters, inasmuch as he had ridden one buffalo to kill another.

Around at the end of the lake our roads diverged. Actually we found very little road as we bore away north and west through pathless forests, across bridgeless streams and past bottomless muskegs for Smoking Lake. Our progress was slow. By the time we reached Mr. Woolsey's, our provisions were about finished. Had he not killed an ox the day we arrived, then we and others would have gone supperless to bed that night. As it was, we had the privilege of chewing at some of the toughest beef I ever tackled. And my experience along that line has been a very wide one.

Mr. Woolsey, his interpreter, and two hired men made up this settlement at the time. One small house and a roofless stable were the only improvements. Mr. Woolsey had begun here within the year, and his difficulties had been neither few nor small. Any Indians who might look upon this place as a future home were now either moose-hunting in the north or out on the plains after buffalo.

Father's plan was that Mr. Woolsey should accompany us out to the rendezvous already arranged for with Mr. Steinhauer and his people. As most of Mr. Woolsey's Indians were out on the plains, he expected to see the people of both missions and the missionaries together.

We struck southward. Mr. Woolsey and his interpreter, William Monckman, made our party up to five. Peter was guide and Father's interpreter. Because of Mr. Woolsey's physical infirmity, we were obliged to travel more slowly than we had thus far. Our road ran along the east side of Smoking Lake and down the creek which runs from the lake to the Saskatchewan. We left most of the ox for the men at the Mission, and had to depend upon our guns for food until we should reach the Indian camp on the plains. We shot some ducks for supper and breakfast the first night out.

Next day we reached the north bank of the Saskatchewan. The appearance of the country around here pleased Father so much that he suggested to Mr. Woolsey the desirability of moving to this place and founding a mission and settlement on the banks of the river. The two missionaries decided that the name of the new mission should be Victoria.

The next move was to cross this wide and swiftly flowing river. No ferryman appeared to answer our hail. No raft or canoe or boat was to be seen, no matter where you might look. Father and Mr. Woolsey had gone to explore the site of the new mission. William was guarding the horses. If we had even a small dugout or log canoe, I would have been at home. Peter was left to bridge the difficulty.

Presently I said, "How are we going to cross?"

"Never you mind," said he. "Do as I tell you."

Soon I received my instructions. They were to go and cut two straight, long green willows about one and a half inches in diameter. I did so, and Peter took these and with them made a hoop. While he was making this, he told me to bring the oilcloth we were carrying with us and to spread it on the beach. Then he placed the hoop in the centre of the oilcloth, and we folded it in onto the hoop from every side. Then we carried our saddles, and blankets, and tent, and kettle, and axe — in short, everything we had, and put them in this hoop.

Then William came and helped us carry this strange thing into the water. To my astonishment it floated nicely. I was told to hold it in the current. Peter, calling to the missionaries, said, "Take off your shoes, gentlemen, and wade out and step into the boat." I could hardly credit this; but the gentlemen did as bidden and very soon were sitting in the hoop. To my greater wonder, it floated.

Peter in the meantime took a "chawed line." This was made of buffalo hide, having been made by cutting some green hide into a strand, about an inch or more wide, and stretching this, and as it dried, scraping the hair and flesh from it. When it was thoroughly dried, the manufacturer began at one end and chewed it through to the other end, and then back again. He continued this until the line was soft and pliable and thoroughly tanned for the purpose. Great care was taken while chewing not to let the saliva touch the line. These lines were in great demand for lassos, lashings, and bridles.

Peter tied one end of this line securely to the rim of the hoop, and tied the other end to a horse's tail. Fastening a leather hobble to the underjaw of the horse, he vaulted on to its back and rode out into the stream. "Let go, John, when the line comes tight," he said. Gently and majestically, like a huge nest, with the two missionaries sitting as eaglets in it, this strange craft floated restfully on the current.

For a moment I stood in amazement. Then the fact that William and I were still on this side made me shout to Peter, "How are we to cross?" By this time he was swimming beside his horse. Back over the water came the one word, "Swim!" Then later, "Drive in the horses and take hold of the tail of one and he will bring you across." I could swim, but when it came to stemming the current of the Saskatchewan, that was another matter.

However, William and I did as our guide ordered, and soon we were drying ourselves on the south bank. Horses and men and kit were all safely landed. The willow pole and our oilcloth had borne our missionaries and guns and ammunition, and the whole of our travelling paraphernalia without wet or loss in any way.

As soon as the backs of our horses were dry, we saddled and packed, and climbing the high bank of the river, proceeded on our journey. Peter cautioned us by saying, "We must keep together as much as possible. There must be no shooting or shouting towards evening. We are now where we may strike a war party at any time." We stopped early for supper, and then went on late, and camped without fire, another precaution against being discovered by the enemy.

Next morning we were away early. Our step was the "all-day jog-trot." We were now reaching open country. We stopped on the south side of Vermilion Creek at noon.

Our whole larder consisted of two small ducks. These were soon cleaned and in the kettle and served, and five hearty men sat around them. Father asked Mr. Woolsey what part of the duck he should help him to. Mr. Woolsey answered, "Oh, give me a leg, and a wing, and a piece of the breast." I quietly suggested to Father to pass him a whole one.

As we picked the duck bones, and as I drank the broth instead of the tea, we held a council. Finally at Father's suggestion it was decided that Peter and I should ride on ahead of the party and hunt. If we were successful, we would camp until Sunday; if not, we would travel.

Peter and I saddled up sooner than the rest, and rode on. I will never forget that afternoon. The day was superb—bright sunshine, fleecy clouds, and an exhilarating atmosphere. Everywhere, above and around us, and before and beneath us, a rich and lovely country—quietly sloping plains, nicely rounded knolls, big hills on whose terraced heights woodland and prairie seemed to have scrambled for space. Lakelets at different altitudes were glistening with the sun rays and sleeping that quiet afternoon as they shone.

As I rode in silence behind my guide, I saw a dark object in the distance, seeming to come out of a bluff of poplars on to the plain. I checked my horse, watched intently for a little and saw it move. I whistled to Peter and pointed to what I saw. "It is a buffalo," he said.

After riding some distance we came to a ridge where Peter declared that what he now saw was a bear and not a buffalo. Carefully scanning the ground he laid his plan for killing it. The bear was lazily coming to the shore of the lake, and Peter said, "I think he is coming to bathe and probably he will swim across to this side of the lake."

There was a gully running down through the hills to the lake. Peter told me to follow that to the shore. He would ride around and thus give us a double chance. We separated and I made my way down the gully. Coming near the lake I dismounted and crawled up the little hill which was my only cover. Parting the grass at the top of the hill, what I saw almost made my heart jump into my mouth. Here was Bruin swimming straight for me!

I crawled back under cover and tried to quiet my nerves and waited my chance to shoot. Then, looking through the grass again, I saw the bear swimming as hard as he could back to the shore he had come from. He was far out, but I tried a shot at him. The ball struck the water just to the left of his head. I saw Peter galloping around the end of the lake to intercept the bear.

Jumping on my horse, I followed as fast as I could and began to load my gun as I rode. This was an entirely new experience for me and took me some time to accomplish. I spilled the powder and got some of it in my eyes. In putting the stopper of my powder-horn — which I held in my teeth — back into the horn, I caught some of the hairs of my young moustache and I felt a pretty smart pain when these were pulled out as the horn dropped and swung down to my side.

During all this I kept my eyes alternately between Peter and the bear; saw the bear reach the shore; saw Peter come close to him; saw Peter's horse plunge, and jump, and kick, and try to run away; saw Peter chance a shot while his horse was thus acting; saw that he tickled the bear's heel; saw the bear grab up its heel and, giving a cry of pain, settle down to run for the nearest woods; heard Peter shout to me, "Hurry, John! Head him off!"

I was coming as fast as my horse could bring me, and thinking, far in advance of my pace, "What shall I do if I catch the bear before he reaches that thicket? My horse may act like Peter's has, and I will miss the bear, as sure as fate."

Just then I saw a lone tree standing on the plain right in the course the bear was taking and it flashed upon me what to do. "I will ride up between the bear and the tree, jump off, let the bear come close, and then if I miss him I will drop my gun and make for that tree."

I felt I could leave the bear in a fair run for that distance. We required the food. And I wanted to kill that bear. With all my heart I wanted to kill that bear. Now I was opposite and my horse began to shy and jump. So, I uncoiled my lariat and let it drag to make it easier to catch him later, and jumping from his back I let him go.

Now the bear saw me between him and the brush. He showed the white of his teeth, put back his ears, and came at me straight. I looked at the tree, measured the distance, cocked my gun, and let him come until he almost touched the muzzle and then fired. Fortunately my bullet went into his brain and down he dropped at my feet. I was for a moment the proudest man in the Northwest.

Mark my astonishment when Peter came at me vehemently. "You young rascal! What made you jump off your horse? That bear might have killed you. It was all an accident, your killing him. Your father put you in my care. If anything had happened to you, what could I say to him?"

I stood there in my folly, yet proud of it. I saw I must change the subject, so I looked innocently at Peter and said, "Do you think he is fat?" Then a smile lit up Peter's face and he said, "Fat! Why, yes, he is shaking with fat." He grasped his knife and laid open the brisket. Sure enough, the fat was there.

As the food supply was now fixed for a day or two, the next question was to bring our party together. Peter told me what to do. "Gallop away to the top of yonder hill and look out for our people. When you see them, ride your horse to and fro until they see you. When they turn toward you, come back to me."

So I galloped away to the distant hill and presently saw our party coming over another. Riding my horse to and fro in a short space, I soon attracted their attention and they turned toward me. When I was sure of the direction I rode back to Peter. By this time he had the bear skinned and cut up. When our folks came to us, we decided to camp there for two days.

We did not carry much when we left. Two days and two nights on fat bear meat straight was quite enough for our party. How often did we think and even say, "If we only had some bread or some potatoes, or anything to eat with this." But there was none.

SEVEN

Among the Plains Cree

We pushed on our way, southeast into the big bend of the Battle River.

In the afternoon we sighted a buffalo. There he stood in his hugeness and ugliness on the plain without any cover. Father and Peter made ready for the race. Father was tremendously excited and rushed around like a boy. First he pulled off his big riding boots and left them on the prairie. He threw down his coat, untied his waterproof from his saddle, and flung that down also. Then putting on a pair of moccasins, he vaulted into the saddle with all the spring and vigour of youth and rode off with Peter.

The bull presently noticed them, lifted up his big, shaggy head, snuffed the air, pawed the ground, and then started. His legs seemed to have no bend in them, and his gait at first was slow, but as the horses came near on the dead run he increased in speed. As he ran he turned his head from side to side to catch a glimpse of his pursuers.

At first I thought I could catch him on foot. Then he spurted and the hunters drove their horses to their best. The brute was too far ahead for them to shoot, and so buffalo and hunters disappeared in the hills from our view and, after them, William.

Only our pack-horses and Mr. Woolsey and I were left. I gathered up boots, coats, and tied them to my saddle. We followed slowly at Mr. Woolsey's pace. "We are lost, John. We may never find our friends again," said my venerable companion. On into the rolling hills we rode and I kept my eye on the spot where I had last seen our friends disappearing. I did wish Mr. Woolsey would come faster. Then I heard voices, and we came up to our hunters and found them skinning the buffalo. Taking some of the meat, we pushed on.

Our guide said we might strike the Indians very soon, for now the whole country gave signs that large herds had recently been roaming and feeding all around. Next day we came to a large trail, indeed to many large trails paralleling each other. A large company in a compact mass had travelled this way. As our party was small, we were constantly on the watch against surprise.

Notwithstanding all our watchfulness, we were surprised in the early afternoon by a troop of Indian cavalry dashing at us from out of the bluff on one side, and another from the other side. With whoops and yells and fine horsemanship they bore down upon us. I did not know what to think. Peter did not seem to mind them. He sat his horse straighter than before. Soon I knew these were friends sent out to escort us into camp. Presently we saw a flag, and coming up over the hill a small body of riders, and in the centre a "kingly-looking man."

"That is Maskepetoon," said Mr. Woolsey.

We dismounted as we met. The chief thanked Father for coming and invoked a blessing on our meeting. They all shook hands and in company with the chief and escort we continued on our way to the camp.

I took stock of the Indians around us and of their horses. The men were fine specimens generally, a large percentage very good-looking. All were armed with either bow and quiver or flint-lock guns. Nearly all were painted—red, yellow, and blue being the chief colours—red predominating. Their costumes varied from a breech-cloth to perforated leather shirts and leggings. Fancy-coloured calico was common for little shirts which were not more than waists and the sleeves of which came a little past the elbow.

Most of the young men had their hair "banged," and I believe that fashion originally came from the plains. Most of them had brass pendants hanging from the hair and ears, as well as brass collars and armlets. Some wore scalp-locks dangling from arm or leg, which not many moons since were the pride of the original owners on whose heads they had grown.

Horses were of all colours and sizes—some very smart and frisky, many exceedingly handsome. The saddles were home-made—some with a bone and wood frame covered with rawhide, others a pad of dressed leather stuffed with moose or deer hair. Stirrups were wood covered with rawhide; stirrup leathers and girths were softened rawhide. Saddle-cloths were home-made too, consisting of the skins of bear, wolf, dog, or buffalo trimmed with strips of red and blue Hudson's Bay strouds—a strong cloth made for this trade.

Many more men had ridden out to meet us, and crowds of boys, two and three on one pony, were joining our *cortège* all the while. The ponies were as full of fun as the boys, many of whom were naked, except for the paint and brass ornaments and beads with which they were bedecked.

We ascended a ridge and saw the large camp before us. There were rings within rings of white tents, varying in size but all of one shape. All were made from the buffalo's hide and many of them were covered with hieroglyphics and paintings indicative either of supernatural power or of martial achievement. Their projecting ventilators, tasselled with buffalo hair, flapped gently in the breeze.

In and out among their tents and beyond them for a mile all around, hundreds of horses were feeding. On almost every knoll groups of guards could be seen whose duty it was to watch over these herds of horses, and the camp also. Everywhere among the tents were stagings made of peeled poles on which was spread the meat of recent hunts in various phases of curing. Here meat was cured without either sugar or salt, but only by the sun and the wind. And either as dried meat, or pemmican, or pounded meat and grease, it will keep for many years.

Women were dressing skins, scraping hides, rendering tallow, pounding meat, making pemmican, slicing up the fresh meat and hanging it on the stages. Some were cooking. Some were sewing with awl for needle and sinew for thread. Scores of naked children were playing and eating and crying in every direction. Hundreds of dogs, half wolf, were fighting and stealing and barking as we rode through the circle of lodges on into the centre of the camp. Here stood a small cluster of large tents.

We alighted. Again the chief welcomed the strangers to his country and camp, once more invoked Heaven's blessings upon the meeting, and then invited us to enter a large tent which was to be our home while in the camp.

Here we found Mr. Steinhauer and his people. This was the first time in the history of the country that three Protestant missionaries had met on the plains. This was the first time in the history of the Methodist Church that a Chairman of a District had visited the Saskatchewan country.

Soon a steaming repast was served of buffalo tongues and "boss." This is the third set or back ribs, unique to the buffalo on this continent. To us this nice, fresh, delicious meat was a feast indeed. We had fed on comparatively nothing, then surfeited on fat bear meat, and made our jaws weary with tough bull meat. But this—no epicure could ask for more or better in the way of meat. Our table was the ground, our mats buffalo robes, our dishes tin. Had we not brought a little salt and tea there would have been none, for the western Indian had not as yet acquired the taste for either. But the kindly manner and princely hospitality, and the delicious quality and large quantity of the meat our hosts served us with, more than made up for anything we might have thought necessary or lacking.

In due time, after our meal was over, the chief asked Father when he would be ready to address his people. Father said that as soon as the camp could be gathered he was ready.

Then the chief summoned two men and said to them, "Ride

forth on either side and shout to my people and say, 'Our friends, the praying men, have arrived. One of them is from afar. He is now about to speak to us words of truth and wisdom. All who can be spared from care of camp and guard of horses, come and listen.'" And the criers went forth and shouted as they rode.

Presently, from the whole circumference of the big camp, throngs of men and women and children gathered to where we were with the chief. The Christians were intensely interested, but the pagans were intensely curious. All were reverent and respectful, for all were religious in their way. Our little company, with the native Christian following, sang some hymns while the crowd gathered. Then the Rev. Mr. Steinhauer prayed.

After that Father began his address. He told of the coming of Jesus, how He had found the world in darkness, and men worshipping idols. He told of the commission given to man to preach the Gospel to every creature and what this Gospel had done for the nations who had accepted it. He showed that true civilization originated in and was caused by Christianity. He said that it was because of the command of Jesus that eastern Christians sent missionaries to the Saskatchewan.

He congratulated them on their country. He foretold the extinction of the buffalo, and the suppression of tribal war, and the necessity of this people's preparing for a great change in their mode and manner of life. It was the business of himself and brethren to teach and prepare them for the change which was bound to come.

He prophesied the ultimate settling of this country. He assured them that the government would do the fair and just thing by them. This had been the history of the British government in her dealings with the Indians, always to do justly and rightly by them.

He congratulated them on having a chief like Maskepetoon, who, while brave and strong, was a lover of peace and earnestly desirous of helping his people in every way. He urged them to listen to him and obey him.

He told them that if God spared his life his purpose was to

come and dwell with them and become one with them in this great country God had given them. He assured them of the profound interest all Christian people had in them, and urged them to have faith in the Great Spirit and in His Son Jesus.

Peter waxed warm and eloquent in his interpreting. He caught the thought and entered into the spirit and purpose of the speaker, and proved himself to be an earnest friend of this people and a prince of interpreters. And that congregation, assembled on the highlands of the continent, under the canopy of heaven—how they listened! No getting up and going away, no restless movements, the instinctive courtesy and reverence and decorum of the natural man was clearly apparent. Civilization does a great deal for man, but it does not always make a gentleman of him.

When the service was over, the chief arose and with quiet dignity spoke to the crowd: "My people, I told you that my friend from the east would speak to you words of wisdom and truth. You have listened to him, and I want you to think of what you have heard. Let this sink into your hearts, for all my friend has said will come to pass. The Great Spirit has sent these praying men to teach us His will.

"Tomorrow we will show our friends our manner of obtaining a livelihood. My runners have brought word that the buffalo are in large numbers nearby, and we will go on a grand hunt tomorrow. Only the necessary guards will remain with the camp.

"Now let the guards be set for tonight, and let there be no recurrence of what took place last night. Someone slept at his post, and the enemy came within the circle of tents, and if he had not been detected, would have stolen and perhaps killed. Shame on the young man who would allow that to happen!

"Go now to your tents, put the camp in order. Remember our friends are tired; they have ridden far. Let there be no unnecessary noise, no drumming or gambling tonight. Let the camp be quiet. Let our friends rest in peace."

When I heard of the great numbers of buffalo and of the grand hunt planned for tomorrow, my whole being was excited with the prospect of witnessing and perhaps participating in it. While

I was wondering how to secure a fresh horse, a young Indian, as if he divined my thought, said to me, "Will you go tomorrow? Will you hunt with us?" I said I would like to and he at once kindly offered me his horse. "Come and see him," said my friend.

I went with him to his tent where he showed me a beautiful little black. The horse was standing near the tent door, eating at a bundle of hay his owner had cut and carried in for him. The lariat around the horse's neck was passed into the door of the tent and fastened near where my friend slept. He evidently was taking extra precaution for the safety of his beloved. I thanked him for his kindness in providing me with a mount.

As I sauntered back to our tent, I took in the scene. Horses were being driven in from all sides. Picket pins were being redriven and made secure. Favourite steeds were being led up to tent doors. Women were busy putting away meat and hides. Others were cooking the evening meal over the flickering campfires. Old men were walking through the camp, urging great caution about horses, and some of them enforcing the advice of the afternoon.

Soon came darkness and quiet. Though tired I could not sleep. My thoughts were busy with all these new experiences, and then the hunt promised for tomorrow kept me awake. When I did sleep, I dreamt of painted savages and buffalo.

EIGHT ⫷⫷⫷

First Hunt

With daylight the camp was astir again. Horses were turned loose under guard. Breakfast was cooked and eaten. Another service was held. Then at the command of the chief, all who could go got ready for the hunt. My friend led up the little black, which looked more beautiful than ever in the morning light. I speedily saddled him and awaited the start in nervous expectancy.

At last the chief mounted, and in company with father and Messrs. Woolsey and Steinhauer led the way. From all parts of the camp riders came forth, many of them leading their runners, so as to have them as fresh as possible for the coming race.

I found myself in the centre of a group of young men and in a little while, without any formal introduction, we were quite acquainted and friendly. They plied me with questions about my previous life, the kind of country I had lived in, and how many people there were. They were astonished when I said there were no buffalo. They were even more astonished when I explained that it was quite possible to live without buffalo. What about war? Did the people where I came from fight?

We rode through prairie and woods. Around us were evidences of the recent presence of thousands of buffalo, the country in some places smelling like a barnyard. Then, after riding some five or six miles, we came upon a ridge which enabled us to look down and across a plain or open country, some ten by twenty miles in size. It seemed to be literally full of buffalo.

The whole country was a black, moving mass. The earth trembled to their tread and roar. Sometimes the clouds of dust from the dustpans as the bulls pawed the earth rose in the air like smoke from a prairie fire. There were thousands of them. My horse became excited with the sight and smell of the great herds. As our line moved down the slope, the outer fringe of buffalo fell back on the larger herds until there seemed to be one living wall before us.

Presently the captain of the hunt gave the command, "Alight! See to your girths and arms, and make ready!"

I watched my companions and as they did, so did I. They tightened their girths and then they began to look to their arms. Most of them had bow and quiver. I turned to one with a gun and watched him. He rubbed his steel and pointed his flint, then took from his ball-pouch some balls, selected some of them, and put these in his mouth. I took several balls from my pouch, selected six, and put them in my mouth. These balls were heavy (twenty-eight to the pound), "but when you are in Rome you must do as Romans do."

In a very short time our captain called, "Mount!"

We formed in one long line. The huge animals moved away as we advanced, increasing their speed as they went. Following our captain, we increased ours. The horses were all excitement; the men were pale, nervous, and quiet. Under foot was rough ground, and there were any number of badger holes. The dangers were being shot, or thrown, or gored. Now we were at half speed, line as yet unbroken.

Suddenly our captain held his gun in the air and shouted, with strong emphasis on the last syllable, "Ah-ah-*how!*"

Away we went, every man for himself. Whips flew. Men were sitting well forward and seemed to go ahead of their steeds. We were in the dust cloud, eyes and ears and nose filled with it. Then we were through and here were the buffalo speeding before us. Already the fast horses were into the herd. The *swish* of an arrow, the blast of old flint-lock, and the wounded animals jumped aside, streams of blood gushing from their nostrils and mouths, showing that they were mortally hit. Others fell dead as soon as shot. Others had either a fore or hind leg broken and stood around at bay challenging another shot. Thus the carnage went on, thicker and faster as the slow-mounted hunters came up.

As for myself, I soon found that six bullets in my mouth were five too many and I slipped the five back into my shot-pouch. Then my horse would spring over several badger holes and my hair would lift; I fancied he would come down in another. When I neared the buffalo, I cocked my gun. In the intensity of excitement and because of an extra jump of my horse, I touched the trigger and off it went—fortunately into the air—and thus I lost my shot. I felt very much mortified at this, but hoped no one would notice what I had done. In fact, all had enough to do in looking after themselves and the game before them.

To load under these conditions is no small matter—horse at full speed, greatly excited, and because of the nature of the ground, now making a plunge, now a short jump, and again a long one. Then a dead buffalo right in the way and your horse jumping over him, another struggling and rising and falling in the throes of death straight ahead of you. Some winded bulls coming athwart your course, heads down and tails up, which you have been told are sure signs of a fight. And to put a climax to the difficulties, you are a tenderfoot, or, as in the Hudson's Bay country dialect, a "greenhorn."

However, after spilling a lot of powder and getting some of it in my eyes, I was loaded at last. Now I saw that the buffalo were driven from me. Just then an Indian chased a cow at an angle towards me, and I also saw that his horse was winded, and I closed in. Yet I did not like to intrude, but the friendly fellow said, "Chase her, my brother," and then I went in gladly. Again he shouted, "That is a good horse you are on. Drive him!" I touched the black with my whip and he speeded. "Drive him!" shouted my friend, "Go close!" And again I struck the black and like the wind he carried me up and I did go close and shot the cow.

Down she dropped and I jumped to the ground beside her, a very proud boy. Ah, thought I, just give me a chance; I will make a hunter as good as the best. My friend came up and said, "You did well, my brother." I thought so too, and though I have killed many hundreds of buffalo since then, and often under far more difficult and trying circumstances, yet that first race and dead-shot can never be forgotten.

My new brother would fain have me take part of the meat. I told him the animal was his, but if he would give me the tongue I would be thankful. This he did, and fastening it to my saddle, I rode on to look over the field of slaughter and to find Father and party if I could.

Ascending a hill, I could see men and women at work skinning and cutting up. In little groups they dotted the plain. The pack-horses were waiting for their loads, and the runners were feeding quietly beside them, their work for the day finished. I think I am within bounds when I say there must have been between eight hundred and a thousand buffalo slain in that run. Many of the hunters killed four, some of them six and seven.

Hunting to kill was considered a small matter, but to kill really good animals was where the skill of the hunter came in. To select a fat one out of scores and hundreds, all on the dead run and mixing as they ran, and to keep your eye on that particular one, watch your horse, load your gun, and look out for wounded and enraged animals in your way, required both skill and nerve. Even among the Indians and mixed bloods born on the plains, there were but few who excelled.

It was late in the afternoon when I found the chief and our party, and I was heartily glad to partake of some dried meat the chief had thoughtfully brought along for the strangers' benefit. Towards evening we were all converging in the direction of the camp and thousands of pounds of meat and many hides were

Paul Kane

Indian Burying Place on the Cowlitz River

being packed home by hundreds of horses. Much of this meat would be eaten, but the greater portion would be cured for future use, or for sale to the Hudson's Bay Company and traders.

In the evening Father again addressed the motley crowd through Peter, and the interest deepened. The days were spent by the missionaries in a succession of services and councils. Then the whole camp moved some twelve or fifteen miles farther east into a still more picturesque and beautiful country. No wonder these people are proud of their birthright, for it is indeed a goodly heritage.

To witness this large camp moving was to me of great interest — the taking down of tents, the saddling and packing of horses and packing of dogs. Both horses and dogs pulled a sort of vehicle made of poles, termed in this country "travois," and thus they both packed and pulled. To these travois the lodge-poles were fastened by the small end and drawn along the ground. Many of the children and the aged and the sick were carried on the travois. Indeed, the carrying and pulling capacity of an Indian pony seemed to be unlimited. Two or three children and a lot of lodge-poles on the travois and the mother and another couple of children on the horse's back. The staunch little fellow ambled along at a quick step, without any trouble or fuss.

When the camp moved, parallel columns were formed and all kept together, the riders and hunters keeping on either side and in front and in the rear. In an incredibly short time the whole camp was in motion. After we came to the spot selected for our new campground, in a very little while tents were up, and stages standing, and meat drying, and work going on as at the other camp. In fact, were it not for the lay of the country one could imagine that the whole village had been lifted from yonder to here without disturbing anything. Long practice and generations of nomadic life had trained the people to constant moving.

Sunday was a special day. The chief's influence and the presence of the missionaries caused the day to be respected by all, irrespective of creed. Prayer meetings and preaching and song services were continued all day, and manifest interest was shown by the people. We had now spent several days with this people and had become acquainted with many of them. I had formed friendships with a number, which, grown stronger with the years, have helped me in my life work ever so much.

Now we must continue our journey. Father told them they might look for him next year about the same time, and as a pledge of this he was going to leave me with Mr. Woolsey in the meantime. Quite a large number escorted us for several miles on our way, and seemed reluctant to have us go. They had provisioned us with the choicest dried meat and pemmican, and our horses were rested and ready to go on.

Our course was now westward up the Battle River, and then northward for Edmonton, or as the Indians termed it, the "Beaver Hill House." As we journeyed we came near the scene of our hunt a few days since. A number of big prairie wolves were to be seen. They were glutting themselves on the offal and carcases left on the field. They were fat and could not run fast, and one could kill them with a club from his horse's back. I drove one up to our party, and Peter and William and I amused ourselves by making him trot between us for quite a distance; then we let him go, for wolf-skins in those days were not worth packing any distance.

We went in by the "Bony Knoll" and what is now known as the "Hay Lake Trail," camped twice, and reached the Saskatchewan opposite the fort in the evening of the third day. Swimming our horses, and crossing in a small boat, we resaddled and repacked and rode into the fort.

We were received kindly by the Hudson's Bay Company's officers and invited to partake of their fare, which was just then pounded meat straight—no bread, no vegetables, nothing else. Pounded meat with marrow fat is very good fare, but alone it becomes monotonous, even before you get through the first meal. The next meal we dined on duck straight. No carving by the gentleman who served. He put a duck on each plate, and we picked the bones clean—at least, I did those of mine.

Edmonton then consisted of the Hudson's Bay Company's fort, and this was all in the vicinity. Out north, about nine miles distant, was a newly commenced Roman Catholic mission. Here, the four walls of the fort enclosed everything. Stores and dwelling houses were packed in a small space, and when the trip-men and *voyageurs* were home for the winter the post would be crowded.

I had now seen three Hudson's Bay Company's forts in the Saskatchewan — Carlton, Pitt, and Edmonton. All were situated in a rich agricultural district, but each and all gave striking evidence that the Hudson's Bay Company was nothing more than a fur-trading organization. They were not settlers or farmers. Pelts and not bread, furs and not homes, were what they aimed at. Though only a boy, I could see that this would be changed. No power under heaven could keep settlement out of this country.

Father was now at his objective point in the west. As the season was advanced, he had to hurry back to Norway House. His plan was to go down the river in a skiff.

I was to remain with Mr. Woolsey as a sort of assistant and interpreter. Mr. Woolsey was to accompany Father in the skiff to where we had crossed the river on our southward journey some weeks before. Peter and I were to take the horses down on the north side to meet them at this point. William had gone to Smoking Lake and would meet us there.

We were to leave Edmonton on the same day, and hoped to reach our rendezvous about the same time. But Peter and I had quite a bunch of horses to drive. Most of the road was dense forest, with the path narrow and almost overgrown with timber. Our horses would run off into the thicket, so that when we came to an open space beyond and counted up, we would generally find some were missing. While I guarded those we had, Peter would go back and patiently track up the rest. Thus, instead of reaching the spot where we were to meet Father and party the second evening, it was long after dark on the third evening when we came there.

I had not seen Father to say good-bye at Edmonton, and I had many things to say to him before we parted for the year. Now I expected to meet him camped on the banks of the river, but as we rode down the hill into the valley all was darkness. There could be no mistake; this was the spot, but there was no camp and no sign of Father. We wondered what was up.

Presently I saw something white, and riding to it I found a note stuck in the end of a small pole. We lit a match and I read:

"MY DEAR BOY, —

"We came here early today and waited some hours, but the season urges me on. Am sorry to miss meeting you. Play the man. Do your best to help Mr. Woolsey.

God bless you, my son. Good-bye.

Your loving father,
G. McDOUGALL."

I learned that Mr. Woolsey and William had gone on towards Smoking Lake, so Peter and I followed and came up with them late at night.

NINE

Apprenticed to Rev. Woolsey

Now I began my service with Mr. Woolsey. Father had suggested two plans for immediate action. One was to send William out to the plains to trade for some provisions. The other was to send me to the site of the new mission, Victoria, and have me make some hay and plough some land for next spring. Mr. Woolsey decided to act on both. We were living on duck and rabbit, and the supply of food was precarious.

William took an Indian as his companion and I took a white man by the name of Gladstone as mine. We travelled together as far as the Saskatchewan, where we took William's carts apart and crossed them over. He and his companion set out to look for provisions.

Gladstone and I started to put up hay and plough the land. For the former we had two scythes, for the latter a coulterless plough, but a tremendously big yoke of oxen. We pitched our lodge down on the bank of the river and went to work. My companion had been a long time in the Hudson's Bay Company's service but was a boat-builder by trade and knew little about either hay-making or ploughing or hunting. However, he was a first-rate fellow, willing always to do his best. He told me that, though he had been in the country for a long time, he had seldom fired a gun and had never set a net.

As we had to hunt our food as well as work, we could not rush things as I wanted to. We had between us a single-barrelled shotgun, percussion-lock, and double-barrelled flint-lock. The first thing we did was to make some floats and put strings on some stones, and I tied up a net we had and we crossed the river and set it in an eddy. Then we fixed up our scythes and started in to cut hay on the ground where we intended to plough. At first our food supply was good. I caught several fine trout in my net and shot some ducks and chickens. We succeeded in making two good-sized stacks of hay.

Then we went to ploughing. It was not until the second day, after a great deal of hard work, that we finally got our oxen to pull together. Then our plough, without a coulter, bothered us tremendously; but we staked out a plot of ground and were determined, if possible, to tear it up. Once our oxen got away and we lost them for three days. "Glad," as I called him, knew very little about tracking, and I very little at that time, but the third day, late in the evening, I came across the huge fellows wallowing in peavine almost up to their backs. Away they went with their tails up, and I had to run my horse to head them off for our tent.

One morning very early I was across looking at my net. We had caught a couple of fine, large trout. Happening to look down the river, I saw men in single file coming along our side, keeping well under the bank. Presently the prow of a boat came swinging into view around the point. The men were tracking her up. I hurried and fixed my net and pulled across and told Glad the news. He was as excited as myself. Isolation is all very fine, but most of us soon get very tired of it. I for one never could understand the fellow who sighed, "Oh, for a lodge in some vast wilderness!"

Very soon the boat came to us, and we found that it contained the chief factor, William Christie, Esq., and his family, and was on its way to Edmonton. Mr. Christie told me about Father passing Carlton in good time some weeks before. He assured me that he would now be safe at home at Norway House.

They had hams of buffalo meat hanging over the prow and stern of their boat. I offered them my fish, hoping they would offer me some buffalo meat. They took my fish gladly, but did not offer us any meat. This was undoubtedly because they did not think of it, or they would have done so; but both Glad and I confessed to each other afterwards our sore disappointment.

However, we ploughed on. We were still three or four days away from our self-set task when as if by mutual agreement, the fish would not be caught, the ducks and geese took flight south, and the chickens left our vicinity. To use a western phrase, "Luck was ag'in us." We had started with two salt buffalo tongues as our outfit when we left Mr. Woolsey. We still had one of these left. We boiled it and ate half the first day of our hard luck. We worked harder and later at our ploughing the second day. We finished the tongue and ploughed on. The third day we finished our task about two o'clock. Then I took my gun and hunted until dark, while Glad gathered and hobbled the horses close to camp. Not a rabbit or duck or chicken did I see.

Glad and I sat beside our campfire that evening and were solemn and quiet. For a week we had been on very short rations. Since yesterday we had worked hard and not tasted any food. We were terribly hungry.

We had hoped that William would have returned before we were through our work; but going on the plains was going into a large country. You might strike the Indian camp soon, or you might be weeks looking for them. And when you found them, they might be worse off for provisions than you were. This all depended on the migrations of the buffalo—sometimes here, and again hundreds of miles away. William might turn up anytime, or it might be a month or six weeks before we heard from him.

Early next morning we took down our tent and packed our stuff. Having the oxen, we went slow. After travelling about ten miles, I saw someone coming towards us. I galloped on to meet him, and found that it was Neils, the Norwegian, who was with Mr. Woolsey. He was on foot, but I saw he had a small pack on his back, and my first question was, "Have you anything to eat?" He said that he had a few boiled tongues on his back. Then I told him that Glad and I were very hungry, and would soon lighten his pack.

Neils told me that Mr. Woolsey had become anxious about us, and at last sent him to see if we were still alive. When Glad came up, we soon showed Neils that our appetites were fully alive. We each took a whole tongue and ate it; then we split another in two and devoured that. And now, in company with Neils, we continued our journey, reaching Mr. Woolsey's the same evening, but making great attempts to lower the lakes and creeks by the way, for after the salt tongue our thirst was intense.

The next thing was to establish a fishery. The buffalo might fail us, and so might the fish; but we must try both. As I happened to be the only one in our party who knew anything about nets and fishing, this work came to me. So I began to overhaul what nets Mr. Woolsey had, and went to work mending and fixing them up. About twenty-five miles north of us was a lake in which a species of whitefish were said to abound, and our plan was to make a road out and give it a fair trial. In the meantime, because of an extra soaking I got in a rainstorm, I had a severe attack of inflammation and, to use another western phrase, had a "close call." But Mr. Woolsey proved to be a capital nurse and doctor combined. He physicked and blistered and poulticed for day and night, and I soon got better. But I was still weak and sore when we started for the lake. I took both Glad and Neils with me. Our plan was to saw lumber and make a boat and then send Glad back. Neils and I would go on with the fishing.

Behold us then started, the invalid of the party on horseback, and Glad and Neils each with an axe in hand, and leading an ox on whose back our whole outfit was packed — buffalo lodge tents, bedding, ammunition, kettles, cups, whipsaw, nails, tools, everything we must have for our enterprise.

These oxen had never been packed before and were a little frisky about it. Several times they made a scattering of things before they settled down to steady work. We had to clear out a great deal of the way and to find this way without any guide or previous knowledge of the place; but our frontier instinct did us good service. Early the third day we came out upon the lake, a beautiful sheet of water surrounded by high, forest-clad hills.

We had with us ten large sleigh dogs and they were hungry. For their sakes as well as our own, we hardly got the packs and saddles off our animals when we set to work to make a raft, man-ufacturing floats and tie-stones, and preparing all for going into the water. Very soon we had the net set. Then we put up our lodge. At once we erected a saw-pit and the men went to work to cut lumber for the boat we had to build.

Before long, in looking out to where we had set the net, I saw that all the floats had disappeared under the water. This indicated that fish were caught, and I got on the raft and poled out to the net. My purpose was to merely overhaul it, and take the fish out, leaving the net set. Very soon I saw that this was impossible. I must take up the net as it was, or else lose the fish; for they would flop off my raft as fast as I took them out of the net. So, I went back to the end of the net and untied it from the stake and took in the whole thing.

Fortunately the net was short and the lake calm. My raft sank below the surface quite a bit and I was up to my knees in water and a living, struggling, slimy mass of fish. They were pulling in all directions. Had they swam in concert, they could have swum away with my raft and me. As it was, I poled slowly to the shore, and shouted to my men to come to the rescue. Soon we had landed between two and three hundred fish. As to quality, not first-class by any means — still, they would serve as dog food and be a guarantee from starvation to man.

While the men were sawing lumber and chopping trees and building the boat, I was busy putting up a stage to hang fish on, and making floats and tying stones, and getting everything ready to go to work in earnest when the boat was finished. This was accomplished the fourth day after we reached the lake. Glad took the oxen and horse and went back to Mr. Woolsey.

Neils and I set our net and settled down to fishing in good

style. We soon found that the lake abounded in worms, or small insects, and these would cling to the net, and if the net was left long in the water, would destroy it, so we had to take it up very often. This with the drying and mending and setting of nets, and making of sticks and hanging of fish, kept us very busy. So far north as we were, and down in the valley, with hills all around us, and at the short-day season, our days were very short. We had to work a lot by campfire, which entailed considerable wood-cutting.

Isolation like ours does not agree with some constitutions. My Norwegian Neils began to become morbid and silent. Long after I rolled myself in my blanket, he would sit over the fire brooding, and I would waken up and find him still sitting as if disconsolate. At last I asked him what was the matter. He told me it was not right for us to be there alone. "You take your gun and go off; what if a bear was to kill you? You will go out in the boat when the lake is rough. If you were to drown, everybody would say, 'Neils did that—he killed him.'"

On the surface I laughed at him, but in my heart was shocked at the fellow, and said, "If anything was to happen to you, would not people think the same of me? We are in the same boat, Neils, but we will hope for the best and do our duty. You and I have been sent here to put up fish. We are trying our best to do so. Let us not borrow trouble."

For a while Neils brightened up. But I watched him.

All of a sudden the lake froze over, and our nets were under, and we had no rope to pass under the ice. So, leaving my gun with Neils who had none, and whistling the dogs to me, I set out on a run for home. It was only twenty-five miles. My intention was to be back in camp the same night, for I could conveniently make a fifty-mile run in those days. Down the valley and over the hills, through the dense forest we went—the ten dogs and myself.

Presently, as we were coasting along the shore of a lake, we met a huge, gaunt timber wolf. I set the dogs on him, but he very soon drove them back and came at me. I remembered seeing some lodge-poles a little way back on the trail. I retreated to them, and securing one, came on to the attack again. Between the dogs and myself, we drove the wolf on to a little point jutting out into the lake, and he took to the ice. I foolishly followed him out, hoping to get a whack at him with my pole, but suddenly I awoke to the fact that the ice was giving way with me and the water was deep. Down I dropped. I stretched out and leaned with the most of my weight on the pole, which, covering a good space of ice, fortunately held me up. So, crawling and pushing, and anxiously looking through the transparent ice for the bottom, I made for the shore. How thankful I was when I did see the bottom and was ashore once more! As I ran off on the trail, I seemed to take a fresh lease on life, for it seemed as if I had nearly lost my grip on it just a few minutes before.

I reached Mr. Woolsey's as he was sitting down to lunch, and he was so glad to see me that he would not hear of my going back that afternoon. A few Indians had come and gone, and from these Mr. Woolsey had secured some dried meat which to me was a great treat after so much fish. We were fast becoming friends, this old bachelor missionary and I. He was as thoroughly good and as kind as men are ever made.

Early the next morning I was away with the rope. By nightfall Neils and I had overhauled several of our nets and put fresh ones in their place.

And now winter set in, with no snow but extreme cold. Neils and I gave our spare time to making a couple of toboggans to take loads of fish home with us. As the ice thickened, the fish went away. We had put up about three thousand. We had lived almost entirely on fish, our only change being the livers of some dogfish and a very few fishducks, which were hardly a change. We had also fattened the ten dogs ready for winter work. We made a strong log cache and put our fish and tents and nets and everything in it.

Having finished our dog sleighs, or toboggans, we contemplated starting in the morning for home, though there was as yet no snow. As it was moonlight, I proposed to Neils that we start at once. So we loaded up, hitched our dogs, and set out. What a time we had — bare ground, fallen timber, stumps and hills. And, to make matters worse, while we were making a fire about midnight to cook our last duck — which we had saved for days for this very meal — the dogs stole it.

Our disappointment was bitter. We had cleaned that duck. We had it all ready to cook. We looked forward to picking its bones ourselves. We craved the change in diet, even if it was only from fish to a fishy duck; but just as we had the prize, the contemptible dogs stole it. Well, we thawed and roasted a fish and started on.

About two o'clock in the morning we came upon a solitary lodge right on the road. It proved to be that of a Wood Stoney, Peter Pe-kah-ches. He and his family were starving. There was no snow, and everything being crisp and crackly with frost, he could not approach game. Peter was a renowned hunter, but the season was against him and thus he was starving. We gave him part of our fish, and received the heart-felt blessings of the whole family, who hardly waited to thaw some of the fish until they ate them.

This lightened our hearts and our loads also, and we went on and reached home before daylight.

TEN

Winter Trips

In the meantime an old drifting kind of man, one of those human beings who seem to be trying to hide away from themselves, had turned up and was domiciled with Mr. Woolsey. He had come across the plains from Fort Garry with a party of white men who grew tired of him and dumped him at Fort Carlton. Then he had gone to Edmonton with the Hudson's Bay Company's carts. There he was thrown out by a rule that no Hudson's Bay officer should allow any stragglers to stay around the post. The penalty was a fine, upon the officer in charge, of ten shillings sterling per day. Someone suggested Mr. Woolsey, and an Indian returning to Fort Pitt was persuaded to bring Mr. O. B. to Mr. Woolsey.

William had come back from the plains, bringing some provisions—not very much, but sufficient to make us all feel thankful. Mr. Woolsey had sent him to Edmonton to bring some horses he had left there, and when he returned he had another "refuge seeker." He was the young son of one of our ministers in Ontario, Williston by name. He had started to cross the mountains with some others, but reaching the Kootanie Pass, their provisions and pluck both dwindled away. They wandered back along the mountains and came to Edmonton in a famished condition. Williston, being "dead-broke," heard of Mr. Woolsey and came down with William. Of course Mr. Woolsey, because of his being the son of a brother minister, took him in.

Now snow came, and Williston and I, each with a dogtrain, made several trips to the lake for fish. These trips were hard work. Besides walking and running all the time over the home stretch, you had to push and pull and strain and hold back to get your load up and down the many hills and over the logs, which were legion and which would have taken more time than we had to clear out of the way.

It was now near Christmas and Mr. Woolsey planned to spend the holidays at Edmonton. This was really his station. For years the minutes of yonder eastern Conference read: "Thomas Woolsey, Edmonton House, Rocky Mountains." Hudson's Bay Company's officers and men came to Edmonton generally for the New Year, and this was the missionary's opportunity of reaching these outposts through these men.

Leaving Mr. O. B. to keep the house warm and William and Neils to saw lumber, the rest of us started for Edmonton. Williston drove the baggage train and I the cariole in which Mr. Woolsey rode. We left long before daylight the Monday morning before Christmas, which came on Thursday that year. We had about four inches of snow to make the road through. This was hardly enough for good sleighing, but where there was prairie or ice our dogs had good footing and made good time. We reached Edmonton Tuesday evening.

That post lived and stood and had its being in the collecting and shipping of furs. A large annual output of the skins and furs of many animals was its highest ambition. Towards this goal, men and dogs and horses and oxen pulled and strained and starved. For this purpose isolation and hardship almost inconceivable were undergone. For the securing and bringing in to Edmonton of the pelts of buffalo and bear, beaver and badger, martin and muskrat, fisher and fox, otter and lynx, the interest of everyone living in the country was enlisted. Thirteen different peoples, speaking eight distinct languages, made this post their periodic centre.

This was the halfway house in crossing the continent. Hundreds of miles of wildness and isolation were on either hand. About midway between and two thousand feet above two great oceans — unique, significant, and alone, without telegraphic or postal communication — thus we found Edmonton in the last days of the last month of the year 1862.

We found the fort full, trappers and traders having returned from their long summer's jouneyings. Here we met with clerks and postmasters from the inland and distant posts. We and they but added to the responsibilities of the head officer, having so many more mouths to feed. Then there were all the dogs, and their food supply was a serious question.

I fully believe that if there was one dog in the small compass of the fort at Edmonton, there were 150. When the bell rang for the men to go to work or come for their rations, the dogs would howl, and one would imagine bedlam let loose. The fights which were taking place at all hours, day or night, became monotonous. The sole topic of conversation would be dogs. The speed and strength and endurance of a dogtrain occupied the thoughts of most men, either sleeping or waking.

Next to the dogs came the dog-runners. These men were famous because of their ability to manage a train of dogs, and the wind and endurance and pluck they manifested in travel. Races were common — five miles, twenty miles, sixty miles, 150 miles, and many of the feats performed by these dogs and dog-drivers would be thought impossible.

We were received very kindly by all parties. I very soon felt at home with such men as R. Hardisty and Mr. MacDonald, and in the family of Mr. Flett, where I received great hospitality. From being a total stranger I was soon made to feel thoroughly intimate.

Mr. Woolsey held service on Christmas morning which was largely attended.

The next day we had dog races and foot races and football, and the fun was fast and furious. It was all especially agreeable to me after the isolation of the last few months, and I was heartily glad Mr. Woolsey had brought me with him to Edmonton. The second day after Christmas was my birthday. I was then twenty years of age.

The second of January, 1863, sees a considerable party of travellers wind out of the gate of the Fort and, descending the hill, take the ice and begin the race down the Big Saskatchewan. Most of our company — with our party a total of eight trains — are old pioneers, full of incident and story of life in the far north, or out on the "Big Plains" to the south. We feed our dogs, we tell our stories, we pile the long logs of wood on our big fire, and alternately change our position, back then front to the fire. We who have been running hard, and whose clothes are wet with perspiration, now become ourselves the clothes-horses whereon to dry these things before we attempt to sleep. Then we sing a hymn, have a word of prayer, and turn in.

The great fire burns down, the stars glitter through the crisp, frosty air, the Aurora dances over our heads and flashes in brilliant colours about our camp, the trees and the ice crack with the intense cold, but we sleep on until between one and two, when we are again astir. Our huge fire once more flings its glare away out through the surrounding trees and into the cold night. After a hot cup of tea, a small chunk of pemmican, a short prayer, and hitching up our dogs, tying up our sled loads and wrapping up our passengers, we are away once more on the ice of this great inland river.

The yelp of a dog as the sharp whip touches him is answered from either forest-clad bank by numbers of coyotes and wolves; but "Marse!" is the word, and on we run, making fast time.

At our turning-off point early in the afternoon, we bade our friends good-bye and, clambering up the north bank of the Saskatchewan, disappeared into the forest. Taking our course straight for Smoking Lake, the whole length of which we travelled on the ice, we climbed the gently sloping hill for two miles and were home again. We had gone 120 miles in less than two days.

Holidays past, we faced our work, which was varied and large: fish to be hauled home; provisions to be sought for, and, when found, traded from the Indians; timber to be got out and hauled some distance; lumber to be "whipped"—that is, cut by the whipsaw; freight to be hauled for Mr. Woolsey, who had some in store or as a loan at Whitefish Lake—all this gave us no time for loitering. Men, horses, dogs, all had to move. Moreover, we had to make our own dog and horse sleds, and sew the harness for both dogs and horses. That for the dogs we made out of tanned moose skins; that for the horses and oxen, out of partly tanned buffalo hide, known as "power flesh," the significance of which I could never comprehend, unless the sewing of them, which was powerfully tedious, was what was meant.

Turn which way you would there was plenty to do. First we hauled the balance of our fish home, then we made a trip to Whitefish Lake and brought the freight which had been left there. Mr. Steinhauer and two of his daughters accompanied us back to Smoking Lake, he to confer with his brother missionary, and the girls to become the pupils of Mr. Woolsey. The opportunity of being taught even the rudiments was exceedingly rare in those days in the North-West, and Mr. Steinhauer was only too glad to take the offer of his brother missionary to help in this way.

About the middle of January we started for the plains to find the Indians and if possible secure provisions and fresh meat from them. William and Neils, with horses and sleds, preceded us some days. Williston and I in the meantime went for the last load of fish, then we followed our men out to the great plains. In those days travelling with horses was tedious. You had to give the animals time to forage in the snow, or they would not stand the trip. From forty to sixty miles per day would be ordinary progress for dogs and drivers, but from ten to twenty would be enough for horses in the deep snow and cold of winter. Thus, although William and Neils had gone ahead, we camped with them our second night out, close beside an old buffalo pound which had been built by the Indians.

It was said by the old Indians that if you took the wood of a pound for your campfire, a storm would be the result. We did take of the wood that night; a storm did come, and William's horses were far away next morning. Williston and I left the most of our little stock of dried meat with the horse party and went on in the storm. Keeping at it all day, we made a considerable distance in a southeasterly direction, where we hoped to fall in with Indians or buffaloes, or possibly a party bent on the same errand as ourselves from the sister mission at Whitefish Lake.

That night both men and dogs ate sparingly. Driving on in the drifting snow, about ten a.m. we came upon a fresh track of dog sleds going in our direction. Closely watching the trail, which was drifting over very fast with the loose snow, we hurried on, and soon came to where these people had camped the night before. We came up to them about the middle of the afternoon. They turned out to be Peter Erasmus and some Indians from Whitefish Lake Mission. Alas, like ourselves they were without provisions.

However, we drove on as fast as we could and had the supreme satisfaction of killing a buffalo cow just before sundown. Very soon the animal was butchered and on our sleds, and finding a suitable clump of timber, we camped for the night. In no time we were roasting and boiling and eating buffalo meat, to the great content of the inner man.

Six hungry, hard-travelled men and twenty-four hungrier and also harder-travelled dogs left very little of that big and fat buffalo cow to carry out of the camp. Supper, or several suppers, for six men and twenty-four dogs and then breakfast for six men and the cow was about gone. But we had pretty good hopes of finding more. We did, and at the end of two days' travel we sighted the smoke of a large camp of Indians.

Nothing special happened during those two days—except that our dogs and an old buffalo bull got badly tangled up and we had to kill the bull to unravel the tangle. It happened in this wise: We started the bull, and he galloped off, almost on our course, so we let our dogs run after him, and the huge clumsy fellow took straight across a frozen lake. Coming upon some glare ice just as the dogs came up to him, he slipped and fell and the dogs and sleds went sliding in all around him. The six trains got tangled up all around the old fellow who snorted and shook his head and kicked but could not get up. We had to kill him to release our dogs and sleds.

The camp we came to had about two hundred lodges, mostly Wood Crees. They were glad to see us and welcomed us right hospitably. We went into Chief Child's tent and made our home there for the short time we were in the camp. But we may be said to have boarded all over this temporary village, for I think I must have had a dozen suppers in as many different tents the first evening of our arrival. While I was eating a titbit of buffalo in one tent, and giving all the items of news from the north I knew, and asking and answering questions, another messenger would come in and tell me he had been sent to take me to another big man's lodge. Thus, until midnight I went from tent to tent, sampling the culinary art of my Indian friends and imparting and receiving information.

I had a long chat with the grand old chief, Maskepetoon; renewed my acquaintance with the sharp-eyed and wiry hunter and warrior, Ka-kate; and made friends with a bright, fine-looking young man who had recently come from a war expedition. He had been shot right through his body, just missing the spine, and was now convalescing.

Next morning we traded for provisions—calfskin bags of pounded meat, cakes of hard tallow, bladders of marrow-fat, bales of dried meat, and buffalo tongues. In a short time Williston and I had all our dogs could haul home.

We had to pack and wrap and lash securely some four hundred pounds of tongues and cakes and bladders of grease and bags of pounded meat on a small toboggan some eight feet by one foot in size. On top of this we tied our own and our dogs' provisions for the return journey, also axe, and kettle, and change of duffels and moccasins. In the meantime we answered a thousand questions that men and women and children who, as they looked on or helped, kept plying us with. By evening we were done.

In the meantime the hunters had been away killing and bringing in meat and robes. With the opening light, and all day long, the women had been busy scraping hides and dressing robes and leather, pounding meat, rendering tallow, chopping bones wherewith to make what was termed "marrow-fat," bringing in wood, besides sewing garments and making and mending moccasins. Only the men who had just come home from a war party, or those who came in the day before with a lot of meat and a number of hides, were the loungers, resting from the heavy fatigues of the chase or war.

We spent another long evening of many invitations and many suppers, of continuous catechism and questionings. Then we had a few hours' sleep, during which the temperature became fearfully cold. With early morn we caught our dogs, who were now rested and who, with what food we gave them and that which they had stolen, had perceptibly fattened.

Our Whitefish Lake friends were ready too, and so we made a start. Our loads were high and heavy. Many an upset took place. To right the load, to hold it back going downhill, to push up the steep hills, to run and walk all the time, to take our turn in breaking the trail—all this soon takes the romance out of winter tripping with dogs. But, we plod on and camp some thirty-five or forty miles out. The already tired drivers must work hard at making camp and cutting and packing wood before this day's work is done; then supper and rest, and prayer and bed, and long before daylight next morning we are away, and by pushing on make from forty to fifty miles our second day.

That night we sent a message back to the Indian camp. The message was about buffaloes of which we had seen quite a number of herds that afternoon. The messenger was a dog. Peter Erasmus had bought a very fine-looking dog from an old woman, and I incidentally heard her, as she was catching the dog, say: "This is now the sixth time I have sold you, and you came home five times. I expect you will do so again." Sure enough, the big fine-looking fellow turned out a fraud. Peter was tired of him, and was about to let him go when I suggested using him to tell the Indians about the buffaloes we had seen. So, a message in syllabics was written and fastened to the dog's neck, and he was let loose. We let him go about eight o'clock at night and before daylight next morning he had made the two days' journey traversed by us. As an Indian would say, "The old woman's medicine is strong."

During the next morning's tramp we separated, each party taking the direct course for home. That afternoon we met William and Neils who had been all this time finding their horses. Surely the spirit of the old structure had been avenged because of our burning some of it; for the storm had come, the horses had been lost, and our men had been in a condition of semi-starvation for some days. We told them where they could find buffaloes and the Indian camp, gave them some provisions, and drove on. We made the old pound the same evening and again made firewood of its walls. To our camp there came that night a tall young Indian. He seemed to resent the desecration of the pound, but our supper and company and news of buffaloes made him forget this for the time. He and two or three others were camped not far off, on their way out to the plains.

Two long days more, with the road very heavy and sometime with no road at all, brought us late the second night to our shack. Mr. Woolsey and Mr. O. B. were delighted to greet us once more. They had been lonely and were anxious about us.

ELEVEN

The New Mission

During that winter the Indians camps at which we could obtain provisions were never nearer than about 150 miles, and sometimes were much farther away. As we intended to build the new mission in the spring, we had to secure lots of supplies. When we had neither flour nor vegetables, animal food alone went fast. So besides hauling food long distances, we had to transport lumber and timber and other material to the new and permanent site on the river bank, some thirty-five miles from where we were. Sometimes with the dog teams we took down a load of lumber to the river and returned the same day. The horses would take from three to four days over the seventy-mile round trip.

One dark morning in February, long before daylight, we saw the flicker of a campfire. We found that it was the one winter packet from the east on its way to Edmonton. Mr. Hardisty, who was in charge of the party, gave me some items of news from the outside world. He also told me that there were letters for Mr. Woolsey and me in the packet, but that this was sealed and could not be opened until they reached Edmonton.

With the first glimmering of day we parted, the winter packet through the deep snow and uncertain trail to Edmonton, we to the Indian camps. In due time we found one of the camps and trading our loads made for home.

I pleaded with Mr. Woolsey to let me go for our mail. Eventually he consented, but said that he could not spare anyone to go with me. I was so eager that I resolved to go alone. My plan was to send Neils and the boy Ephraim out for more provisions and to accompany them as far as the spot where we had seen Mr. Hardisty two weeks before. Then I would follow the packet trail to Edmonton. Mr. Woolsey very reluctantly agreed to all this.

About three o'clock one dark cloudy morning I bid Neils and Ephraim good-bye, put on my snowshoes, and took the now more or less covered trail of the packet men. I had about 250 pounds of ammunition and tobacco that Mr. Woolsey had borrowed from the Hudson's Bay Company and was now returning by me.

I had great faith in my lead dog, Draffan, a fine big black fellow whose sleek coat had given him his name, "Fine-cloth." In fact all four of my dogs were noble creatures. Away we went, Draffan smelling and feeling out the very indistinct trail and I running behind on snowshoes. It was my first trip alone and I could not repress a feeling of isolation. The "letters from home" were constantly in my thoughts and spurring me on. In the waning light of that day I saw the wings or fans of the old windmill which stood on the hill back of Fort Edmonton. Just as the guard was about to shut the eastern gate, we dashed in and were at our journey's end. I had covered a round hundred miles.

Right glad I was at being thus relieved from camping alone that night. With my letters all cheering, and the kind friends of the place, I thoroughly enjoyed the hospitality of Old Fort Edmonton. It was Friday night when I reached the Fort and I spent Saturday and Sunday with the Hudson's Bay officers and men.

I started on my return trip Monday about 10:30 a.m. and by night had made the camp where I had lunched on the way out. To some extent I had got over the shrinking from being alone. I chopped and carried wood for my camp, made myself as comfortable as I could, fed my dogs, and listened to the chorus of wolves and coyotes as they howled dismally around me. Then the wind got up, and with gusts of wild fury came whistling through the trees which composed the little bluff in which I was camped. Soon it began to drift, so I turned up my sled on its edge to the windward, and stretching my feet to the fire, wrapped myself in buffalo and blanket and went to sleep.

When I awoke I jumped up and made a fire and looking at my watch saw that it was two o'clock. The wind had become a storm. I went out of the woods to where I thought the trail should be and felt for it with my feet. There under the newly drifted snow was the frozen track. I thought that if I could start Draffan right, he would be likely with his wonderful instinct to keep on course. I then went back to the camp and harnessed my dogs. As I had little or no load, I made an improvised cariole or what was termed a "Berlin" out of my wrapper and sled lashings.

The storm was now raging, the night was wild, and the cold was intense. Wrapped in my warm robe, I stretched myself in the "Berlin" and got as flat as possible in order to lessen the chances of upsetting. When ready I gave the word to Draffan, saw that he took the right direction, and then covering up went to sleep. With sublime faith in that dog I slept on. If I woke up for a moment, I merely listened for the jingle of my dog-bells, and by the sound satisfied myself that my team were travelling steadily, and then went to sleep again.

On the way out I had noticed a long side hill. Now I said to myself, "If we are on the right track, I will surely upset at that point." Sure enough I did wake up to find myself rolling, robe and all, down the slope of the hill. I jumped up, shook myself and the robe, righted the sled, stretched the robe into it, and then giving my leader a caress and a word of encouragement, I put on my snowshoes and away we went at a good run. We kept it up until daylight, when we stopped. I unharnessed the dogs, made a fire, boiled my kettle and had breakfast.

Now we were on familiar ground. I was so elated at having successfully made the trip up to this point that I could not sit still very long, but running and riding kept on. We did not stop for lunch. The early dusk of the stormy day found us at the southerly end of Smoking Lake and some twelve or fifteen miles from home. Again I wrapped myself in my robe and, lying flat in the sled, felt I could very safely leave the rest to old Draffan and a kind Providence and go to sleep. I woke up as the dogs were climbing the steep little bank at the north end of the lake. Then a run of two miles and I was home again.

With the first tinkle of my dog-bells Mr. Woolsey was out, peering into the darkness and shouting, "Is that you, John?" My answer, he assured me, filled him with joy. He took me in his arms and almost wept over me. He brought dogs, sled and my whole outfit into the house. The kind-hearted old man had passed a period of great anxiety. He had been sorry a thousand times that he had consented to my going to Edmonton, had dreamed of my being lost or of my bleeding to death or of my freezing stiff.

He did not ask for his mail, did not think of it for a long time, so thankful was he that the boy left in his care had come back to him safe and sound. I was glad to be home again too. The uncertain road, the long distance, the deep snow, the continuous drifting storm, the awful loneliness, were all past. I had found Edmonton, had brought the mail, was home again beside our own cheery fire, and was a proud and happy boy.

In a day or two Neils and Ephraim came in from the camp. Once more we made another start for provisions and later on yet another, never finding the Indians in the same place. We were successful in reaching their camps and in securing loads. So, my first winter on the Saskatchewan gave me the opportunity of covering a large portion of the country and becoming acquainted with a goodly number of the Indian people. I had also constant practice in the language, and was now quite familiar with it.

Some time in March, Mr. Woolsey, wishing to confer with his brother missionary, Mr. Steinhauer, decided to go to Whitefish Lake and to take the Steinhauer girls home at the same time. Mr. and Mrs. Steinhauer were delighted to have their daughters home and glad to have a visit from us. We spent two very pleasant days with these worthy people.

With the approach of spring we prepared to move down to the river. We put up a couple of stagings and also a couple of buffalo-skin lodges, in one of which Mr. Woolsey and Mr. O.B. took up their abode, while the rest of our party kept on the road bringing down from the old place our goods and chattels, lumber and timber.

As the days grew warmer, we who were handling dogs had to travel most of the time in the night, as then the snow and track were frozen. While the snow lasted, we slept and rested during the warm hours of the day. In the cool of the morning and evening and all night long we kept at work transporting our materials to the site of the new mission. The last of the season is a hard time for the dog-driver: the night work; the glare or reflection of the snow by sun and moonlight; the settling of the snow on either side of the road which caused constant upsetting of sleds; the melting of the snow which made your feet wet and sloppy almost all the time — these were the inevitable experiences.

The snow had almost disappeared and the first geese and ducks were beginning to arrive when suddenly one evening Mr. Steinhauer and Peter Erasmus turned up, *en route* to Edmonton. Mr. Woolsey took me to one side and said, "John, I am about tired of Mr. O. B. Could you not take him to Edmonton and leave him there? You might join this party now going there."

When we reached Edmonton I was glad to transfer my charge to someone else's care. I was not particular who took him, for like Mr. Woolsey I was tired of the old fraud.

The Chief Factor said to me that evening, "So you brought Mr. O. B. to Edmonton. You will have to pay ten shillings for every day he remains in the Fort."

"Excuse me, sir," I answered, "I brought him to the foot of the hill, down at the landing, and left him there. If he comes into the Fort I am not responsible."

Shortly after this Lord Milton and Dr. Cheadle came along on their way to the Pacific, and Mr. O. B. joined their party. These gentlemen wrote a book descriptive of their journey and in this Mr. O. B. appears. I am done with him.

Spring was now open, the snow nearly gone, and we had to make our way back from Edmonton as best we could. I cached the cariole, hired a horse, packed him with my dog harness, blankets, and food, and thus reached Victoria. My dogs, having worked faithfully for many months and having travelled some thousands of miles, sometimes under most trying circumstances, were now entering upon their summer vacation. How they gambolled and ran and hunted as they journeyed homeward!

With the opening spring Indians began to come in from the plains, and for several weeks we had hundreds of lodges beside us. Mr. Woolsey was kept busy holding meetings, attending councils, visiting the sick, acting as doctor and surgeon, magistrate, and judge. A number of them had accepted Christianity, but the majority were still pagan. These were full of curiosity as to the missionary and his work, and keenly watching every move of the "praying man" and his party. The preacher may preach ever so good, but he himself is to these people the exponent of what he preaches, and by him they judge the Gospel he presents. If he fails to measure up in manliness and liberality and general manhood, then they think there is no more use in listening to his teaching.

A few weeks sufficed to consume all the provisions the Indians had brought with them, and a very large part of ours also. So the tents were furled, the people recrossed the Saskatchewan and, ascending the steep hill, disappeared from our view to seek the buffalo away out on the plains. Though we had visits from small bands, coming and going all summer, the larger camps did not return until the autumn.

While Mr. Woolsey was constantly at work among the people, the rest of us were fencing and planting a field, whipsawing lumber, taking out timber to the river, and rafting it down to the mission. We were also building a house. All this time we were living in skin lodges.

Mr. Woolsey aimed at putting up a large house, in the old-fashioned Hudson's Bay style — a frame of timber, with grooved posts in which tenoned logs were fitted into ten-foot spans — and as all the work of sawing and planing had to be done by hand, the progress was slow. My idea was to face long timber and put up a solid blockhouse, which could be done so much more easily and quickly and would be stronger in the end; but I was over-ruled. So we went on more slowly with the big house, and were smoked and sweltered in the tents all summer. However, taking out timber and rafting it down the river took up a lot of my time.

We had to have lumber to make anything like a house for semi-civilized men and women to dwell in. In my humble judgement, the hardest labour of a physical kind one could engage in is dog-driving, and the next to that whipsawing lumber. I have had to engage in all manner of work necessary to the establishing of a settlement in a new country, but found nothing harder.

Our principal food that summer was pemmican or dried meat. We had neither flour nor vegetables. Sometimes, for a change, we lived on ducks, and again varied our diet with duck eggs. We would boil the large stock ducks whole and each person would take one, so that the individual occupying the head of the table was put to no trouble in carving. Each man in his own style did his own carving, and picked the bones clean at that. Then, another time, we would sit down to boiled duck eggs, many a dozen of these before us, and in all stages of incubation. While the older hands seemed to relish these, it took some time for me to learn that an egg slightly addled is very much improved in taste.

Our horses often gave us a lot of trouble because of the extent of their range. Many a long ride I had looking them up. On one of these expeditions I was accompanied by an Indian boy. Having struck the track, we kept on through the thickets and around lakes and swamps until after a while we became very hungry. As we had no gun with us, the question arose: How were we to procure anything for food? My boy suggested hunting for eggs. I replied, "We cannot eat them raw." He answered, "We will cook them."

So, we unsaddled and haltered our horses, and stripping off our clothes waded out into the rushes and grasses of the little lake nearby. We soon found some eggs. While I made the fire, my companion proceeded with what was to me a new mode of cooking eggs. He took the bark off a young poplar and made of this a long tube, tying or hooping it with willow bark. Then he stopped up one end with mud from the lake shore. As the hollow of the tube was about the diameter of the largest egg we had, he very soon had it full of eggs. Stopping up the other end also with mud, he moved the embers from the centre of the fire, laid the tube in the hot earth, covered it over with ashes and coals. In a few minutes we had a deliciously cooked lunch of wild duck eggs. I had learned another lesson in culinary science.

In the midst of our building and manufacture of timber and lumber, rafting and hauling, fencing and planting, weeding and hoeing, every little while there would come in from the plains rumours of horse-stealing and scalp-taking. The southern Indians were coming north, and the northern Indians going south. We did not expect any attack because we were so far north and because the Indian camps were between us and our enemies. Still, we felt it prudent to keep a sharp lookout and to conceal our horses as much as possible by keeping them some distance from where we lived. All this caused considerable riding and work and worry, and kept us busy late and early.

About the end of July, the "Summer Brigade," made up of several inland boats, left Edmonton manned by men who had been on the plains, and passed us on its way to Fort Carlton. There it would meet the regular brigades from Norway House and York Factory, and the overland transport from Fort Garry which came by oxcarts. Mr. Hardisty was with the boats, and he invited me to join him until he should meet the boats in which my father and mother had taken passage from Norway House. Mr. Woolsey kindly consented to let me go.

The river was almost at flood-tide, so we made very quick time. Seven or eight big oars in the hands of those hardy voyageurs, backed by the rapid swirl of this mighty glacier-fed current, sent us sweeping around point after point and along the lengths of majestic bends. At night our boats were tied together, and one or two men kept the whole in the current while the others slept. At meal times we put ashore for a few minutes while the kettles were boiled and then, letting the boats drift, we ate our meal *en route*.

Early in the middle of the second afternoon we sighted two boats tracking up the southerly bank of the river. My people were with them. The Hudson's Bay Company had kindly loaded two boats and sent them on from Carlton, in advance of the brigade, so that Father and family should have no delay in reaching their future home. Thanking my friend Hardisty for the very pleasant run of two hundred miles he had given me with him, I transferred to the boat Father and Mother and my brother and sisters were in. We were very glad to meet again. My sisters were sunburnt, sturdy, happy girls and my baby brother had grown and was toddling around like a little man.

Mother was looking forward eagerly to the end of the journey. Already it had occupied a month and more on the way up. Half of that time had been in the low country, where water and swamp and muskeg predominate; where flies and mosquitoes flourish and prosper, and reproduce in countless millions; where the sun in the long days of June and July sends an almost unsufferable heat down on the river as it winds its way between low, forest-covered banks. The carpenter, Larsen, whom my father was bringing from Norway House, met with an accident through the careless handling of his gun, and for days and nights Mother had to help in nursing and caring for the poor fellow. No wonder she was anxious to reach Victoria and have a change and a rest.

Only a day or two before I met them, my folks had the unique sight of witnessing the crossing through the river of thousands of buffalo. The boatmen killed several, and for the time being we were well supplied with fresh meat.

Our progress now was very much different to mine coming down. The men kept up a steady tramp, tramp on the bank at the end of seventy-five or one hundred yards of rope from the boat.

Four sturdy fellows in turn kept it up all day, rain or shine. Though our headway was regular, yet because of the interminable windings of the shore, we did not seem to go very far in a day. Several times Father and I took across country with our guns and brought in some ducks and chickens; but the unceasing tramp of the boats' crews did not allow of our going very far from the river.

I think it was the tenth day from my leaving Victoria that I was back again, and Mr. Woolsey welcomed his chairman and colleague with great joy. Mother was not loath to change the York boat for the large buffalo-skin lodge on the banks of the Saskatchewan. The first thing we went at was hay-making on the old plan, with snath and scythe and wooden forks. As the weather was propitious, we soon had a nice lot of hay put up in good shape.

Father saw at once that the house we were building would take a long time to finish, and as we had some timber in the round in hand, he proposed to put up at once a temporary dwelling house and a storehouse. At this work we went, and Mr. Woolsey looked on in surprise to see these buildings go up as by magic. It was a revelation to him, and to others, the way a man trained in the thick woods of Ontario handled his axe. Without question, Father was one of the best all-purpose axemen I ever knew.

Then Father sent me up the river with some men to take out timber and to manufacture some lumber for a small church. While we were away on this business, Father and Larsen were engaged in putting the roof on, laying the floors, putting in windows and doors to the log house, and otherwise getting it ready for occupancy. Despatch was needed, for while a skin lodge may be passable enough for summer, it is a wretchedly cold place in winter, and Father was anxious to have Mother and the children fairly housed before the cold weather set in.

In the meantime Peter Erasmus had joined our party as Father's interpreter and general assistant, and was well to the front in all matters pertaining to the organization of the new mission.

TWELVE

Gospel Riders

Father had been disappointed at not seeing the Mountain Stoneys on his previous trip west. Now, with the temporary house finished, the hay made, and other work well on, and as it was still too early to strike out on the fresh meat hunt, he decided to make a trip with Peter as guide into the Stoney Indian country.

Accordingly, one Friday morning early in September, Father and Peter and I set out. We took the bridle trail on the north side of the Saskatchewan and reached Edmonton on Saturday evening. Father held two services on Sunday in the officers' mess room, both well attended.

Monday morning we crossed the river and struck southwards on the "Blackfoot Trail." Next day we left the trail and started across country, our course being due south. The following evening found us at the Red Deer.

Here we saw the first signs of Stoneys. The Stoneys made an entirely different trail from that of the Plains Indians. The latter left a broad road because of the *travois* on both dogs and horses, and because of dragging their lodge-poles with them wherever they went. The Stoneys had neither lodge-poles nor *travois*, and generally kept in single file, thus making a small, narrow trail.

Sometimes, depending on the nature of the ground, it was very difficult to trace.

The signs indicated that these Indians had gone up the north side of the Red Deer River. We followed them through a densely wooded country, back to the river and over it eastward into a range of hills, and then down into the canyon of the Red Deer.

The banks were high and in some places the view was magnificent. In the long ages past, the then mighty river had burst its way through these hills and had in time worn its course down to the bedrock. In doing so it left valleys and flats and canyons to mark its work. We burned out our frying pan and prospected for gold. We found a quantity of colours. But, as this was a dangerous country, it being the theatre of constant tribal war, a small party would not be safe to work here very long.

We moved camp out of the canyon up to near the mouth of the Blind Man's River. Father's and Peter's plan was to come out at a place on our outbound trail which we had named Goose Lake because of having dined on goose there. We reached it about midday. Saturday afternoon we crossed Battle River.

Most of the time we had been living on our guns. In starting we had a small quantity of flour. About two pounds was now left. Our intention was not to travel on Sunday, if we could in the meantime obtain a supply of food. At the "Leavings," where the trail in after years between Edmonton and Southern Alberta touched and left the Battle River, I saw a fine flock of stock ducks. Firing into them, I brought down two. Almost immediately I heard the report of a gun away down the river.

Father called to me, "Did you hear that?" I said, "Yes." Then he said, "Fire off the second barrel in answer." Which I did, and there came over the hill the sound of another shot. Peter came up greatly excited, asking us if we had heard the shots. We explained that two came from us, and the others from parties as yet unknown. "Then," said he, "we will tie our horses and be ready for either friends or foes."

Presently we were hailed from the other bank of the river. We saw two Indians peering from out the bush. They came across and proved to be Stoneys. Both were fine-looking men. Their long black hair hung pendant in two neat braids down their breasts. The middle tuft was tied up off the forehead by small strings of ermine skin. Their necks were encircled with a string of beads, with a sea-shell immediately under the chin. They were strong and well built, with immense muscular development in the lower limbs, showing that they spent most of their time on their feet and had climbed many a mountain and hill. Thrown over their shoulders as they crossed the river were a thin, neatly made leather shirt, a breech-cloth, fringed leather leggings, and moccasins.

Away bounded our visitors when they heard that the missionary and his party were going to stay some time with them and their people. In a very short time our camp was a busy scene of men, women and children, dogs and horses. Provisions poured in on us, and our commissariat was secure for that trip. To hold meetings, to ask and answer questions, to sit up late around the open campfire in the business of the Master, to get up early Sunday morning and hold services and catechize and instruct all the day until bedtime came again was the constant occupation and joy of the missionary. No man I ever travelled with seemed to enter into such work and be better fitted for it than my father. Though he never attempted to speak in the language of the Indian, yet few men knew how to use an interpreter as he did. And Peter was no ordinary interpreter.

These Indians told us that the Mountain Stoneys were away south at the time, and that there would be no chance of our seeing them on this trip. In all probability they would see the Mountain Indians during the coming winter and would gladly carry to them any messages that Father might have to send. The best site for a mission was discussed; it was desirable to have the location central for Mountain and Wood Stoneys. The oldest man in the party suggested Battle River Lake, the head of the stream on which we were encamped, so Father determined to take this man as guide and explore the lake. Monday morning found us early away, after public prayer with the camp, to follow up the river to its source. We were three days of steady travelling on this side trip.

After two more services with this interesting people, and bidding them good-bye, we started home. Going down Battle River, we passed outside the Beaver Hills, skirted Beaver Lake, and passing through great herds of buffalo without firing a shot — because we had provisions given us by the Indians — we found ourselves, at dusk Saturday night, about thirty-five miles from Victoria. Continuing our journey until after midnight, we unsaddled and waited for the Sabbath morning light to go on into the mission.

About the first of October we organized our party for the plains. There was a lot of work to do — horses to hunt up, carts to mend, old axles to replace, harness to fix. We had one waggon. The rest of our vehicles were of the Red River pattern, wood through and through, that screamed as it rolled. Some of these wanted new felloes, and others new spokes, one a new shaft.

When all was ready, we had the river to cross, and our only means of ferriage was a small skiff. This involved many trips. Then came the work of swimming our stock across. With the horses we had little difficulty, but the oxen were loath to take the water, and we had to lead them over one by one. When all were across and hitched up, we had the big hill to climb. We had to double our teams to take a light cart to the summit, for the south bank is almost perpendicular.

Father was captain of the hunting party, with Erasmus second in command. The rest of us were teamsters or guards or privates, as the need might be. Mr. Woolsey stayed behind in charge of the mission. On the second day out we met the vanguard of Maskepetoon's camp on their way to the mission. From them we learned the glad news that we might expect to find buffalo about the fifth day out.

Our rate of travel was governed by the oxen. In going out I drove the waggon and went ahead. Our "runners" ran and fed beside us as we travelled. These we seldom touched on the journey, except to give them a short run by way of exercise and to

Two Assiniboine Indians Running a Buffalo

keep them in wind. Father and Peter were in the saddle, and drove up the loose stock, or were anywhere on the line of march as might be required.

About the middle of the afternoon of the second day out, we met Maskepetoon himself. He was delighted to see Father again, and said he would send some of his young men with us to help in the hunt and to help guard our camp and party. The old gentleman got into my waggon to ride to where the Indians were.

Presently I saw an old man of singular appearance coming towards us. Maskepetoon turned the other way, which I thought strange. The old man came up to my side of the waggon and said, "I am glad to see you, young white man."

The chief still kept his face turned away. I saw, however, that after shaking my hand, the old man would also shake hands with my companion, so I nudged Maskepetoon and said, "This man wants to shake hands with you." Then the chief, as if jerking himself from under a weight or strain, turned and gave his hand to the old fellow who grasped it and uttered the Indian form of thanksgiving.

It was some time before Maskepetoon spoke to me again. "John, that man killed my son, and I have often longed to kill him. But because I have wanted to embrace the Christian religion, I have with great effort kept from avenging my son's murder. I have never spoken to him or shaken hands with him until now. Meeting your father and sitting beside you has softened my heart, and now I have given him my hand. It was a hard thing to do, but it is done, and he need fear no longer so far as I am concerned."

Maskepetoon sent four of his people with us — his son Joseph, his nephew Jack, a Blood man, and a Swamptree — fine fellows every one of them. Joseph was big, solid and staid, a man you could depend on. Jack was small, quick and wild, fond of war and given to excess. The Blood and the Swamptree were pagans still, but instinctively kind and well disposed.

The Blood man was under vows to his "familiar spirit," or "the one he dreams of," and one of the commands given to him was to give a whoop every little while, a very peculiar semi-peace, semi-war whoop. He said to me, in confidence, "John, you do not mind me, but I dare not make my whoop before your father. That is why I go away from camp now and then. I must whoop; it would choke me, kill me, if I did not." I told him to "whoop it up." I saw no harm in it and he was comforted.

The Swamptree, on the fourth day out, was riding in the waggon with Father and me. We were passing through bluffs of timber, thickly dotting the prairie. Suddenly I saw the Swamptree string his bow and throw an arrow into position in a flash. Looking to where he indicated I caught the glint of an eye. Our guns were soon brought to bear on a crouching Indian who, seeing he was discovered, rose with his hand up. He and a companion were camped for dinner on the other side of the bluff of timber. They had heard us coming and were bound to make sure who we were before showing themselves.

Next day about noon we sighted buffalo in "bunches" or bands. The country was rolling and half prairie and half bush. Jack and Joseph and Peter and I saddled and made ready to run. We charged at the buffalo as they were running down the slope of a hill towards an opening between two dense thickets of timber. The last I saw of Peter was when two bands of buffalo were meeting in their mad rush for this opening. His horse, old Ki-you-ken-os, a big bay that had evidently been stolen from the Americans to the south, had been brought into Edmonton by a Blackfoot and had come into Mr. Woolsey's hands. It was a fine animal, but altogether too impetuous and strong-mouthed to make a good buffalo horse. Ki-you-ken-os seemed determined to take the gap before the buffalo.

Peter had his gun stuck in his belt, had hold of the double reins from the big curb-bit with both hands, and was pulling with all his might, mouth wide open, and eyes bulging out. But the old horse did not seem to heed either Peter or his bit—he was running the buffalo a race for yonder gap.

I was terribly anxious for Peter. In a few moments the two herds came against each other. A moment later the horse and his rider were in the centre of the confused mass, and then all I could see was buffalo stampeding, and old Ki-you-ken-os leaping over and running amongst the wild herd which was now tightly jamming its way through the narrow prairie lane. Perhaps four hundred buffalo were there. Dust and distance hid the scene from me.

Peter and I did not kill in this race. Indeed, he was thankful, as was I, that he was not killed. But Joseph and Jack made up for it, and we were busy all the rest of the evening butchering and hauling in to camp.

We were now in the short day and long night season, and the nights were cold, so we had to have a big campfire. We got well down between the bluffs, in order that the glare of our fire would be hidden as much as possible, and arranged our carts around the camp so that these would act as a kind of barricade in case of attack.

Supper took hours to get through, for everybody had his choice bit to roast. The cook for the evening would have a whole side of ribs swinging before the fire, and when these were cooked the ribs were parted along the whole length, and each man took one. When he had picked it clean he either turned his attention to his own independent roast, or took another rib. One had brought the head in, though generally when you took the tongue out you left the head for the wolves. Another had two or three fathoms of entrails, which he cleaned with fire, and then roasted, and cutting them up in lengths, passed these around to his friends. Another had a large piece of the stomach or tripe, which he also cleaned with fire, and relished as a favorite morsel. Still another was cracking marrow bones and eating the marrow. Thus supper was prolonged far beyond the usual time.

When those whose turn it was to sleep felt it was bedtime, we would sing a hymn, and father would lead in prayer, then the bed-making began. With old hands this commenced by piling saddles and camp equipment or logs of wood behind the head and on each side of where you were going to sleep. Experience had taught these wary fellows that many a bullet and arrow had been stopped, or made to glance off, by such simple precautions. Fresh guards set, the rest lay down with clothes and moccasins on so as to be ready to jump up at any time.

The next day we finished loading and started homewards. We were back at the Saskatchewan thirteen days after leaving the mission.

A great change had come over the place since we had left. Hundreds of lodges now dotted the valley, and Mr. Woolsey and Maskepetoon had been very busy keeping the camp in order. A great many Plains Crees were here mixed up with our quieter Wood Crees, and war parties were coming and going all the time. Mother and my sisters, though among Indians for many years — in fact the girls had spent all their lives among them — had never seen anything like this before. Men and women would crowd around the little temporary mission house, and in full savage costume, and with faces painted in divers colours, peer into the windows, and darken the door, and look with the greatest curiosity on the white woman and her children.

Paganism was rife. Conjuring and gambling were going on night and day. Dance feasts, and dog feasts, and wolf feasts, and new lodge dedication feasts were everyday occurrences. I was invited to join in one of the latter by a Plains Cree, a warrior and a polygamist and a dandy of the first circle, who had taken a fancy for me. His name was peculiar, but he, being a sleek and fine-looking fellow, most certainly belied it. "The Starving Young Bull" was the gentleman who honoured me with an invitation to be present at the dedication feast of his new lodge, now about finished. These new lodges were gorgeous things in their way. The twenty or more buffalo skins had been dressed as soft and white as possible and then cut into shape by some pattern carried in the brain of one of the older women. Then at a bee of women, where also a feast was provided, the skins were sewn together with the sinews of the buffalo. When the new tent, tasseled with the tail of the same animal, was fully set, then the artist friends or the proprietor himself went to work to paint on its outside walls the achievements of the warrior and hunter.

There might be scenes of plunder, blood, military prowess or medicinal lore, so that on approaching a tent you could read the degree and dignity of the man you were about to visit.

I accepted Mr. Starving Young Bull's kind invitation and was on hand at the time he had indicated. "Just as the day is departing," was the hour he fixed. There may have been forty or more guests. We sat in a ring around the tent. Each man had before him his own dish which he had brought with him. When these had been heaped up with buffalo dainties and dried berries, four old conjurers who sat at the head of the tent, each dressed in accord with the instructions of the "spirit of his dream," now began the dedication service.

First, the oldest conjurer took the big medicine pipe with the long stem. This had been previously filled, and as he solemnly held it in both hands, another with his knife placed a live coal on the contents of the pipe. This done, the old man pulled at it until it was fairly alight, and then held the stem heavenwards, at the same time muttering what to us were unintelligible sounds. Next he pointed the stem to the earth, then slowly moved it around with the sun, and taking another whiff or two, passed it to his fellow conjurers, who each in turn took long pulls at the big pipe. After this the four took their sacred rattles and began to sing and incant, keeping time with the rattles. Then they all began to speak in an unknown language, or as it is literally translated, "using a different language."

When through with this, the old man in the language of the people offered up a prayer, or rather expressed a wish: "that this tent might be blessed; that its occupants might be prospered; that the owner, in his going and coming in, whether for hunting or war, might be successful; that the kettles of the women of this tent might always boil with plenty; that the pipe of the owner might always be full." All was responded to by the guests. Then we devoted ourselves to the feast, eating much or little as we chose, and taking home with us what we did not eat.

In the midst of all these old institutions and rites, which these people had been bred in for centuries our missionaries were hard at work. Meetings and councils followed each other in quick succession, and early and late Father and Mr. Woolsey were busy preaching the Gospel of Christianity and civilization to these men to whom they had been sent.

THIRTEEN

Supporting Victoria

Meanwhile, we were putting up stables and out-buildings and going on with work on the mission house. We also put up the walls of a small church.

Upon me fell the work of establishing the fall fishery, and to me was given as companion and fellow worker a young Canadian, Thomas Kernan by name. Our plan was to go down the river in the skiff as far as the Snake Hills, which were about opposite Saddle Lake, and then portage our boat over the hills the eight or ten miles to the lake. Peter was to meet us at the place of landing, and we took with us in our boat a pair of cartwheels on which to transport our boat from the river to the lake. An axe and an auger were all the tools we had. We took a skin lodge to live in at the fishery.

Embarking one afternoon, we came to the place of meeting early the next day. Peter turned up in convenient time with a horse, and we went to work to make a frame and axle for the wheels. Soon we had our boat loaded on this with our fishing outfit, tent, and were tramping up the hills. We were at the lake in time to put up our tent and set one net that night. Peter returned home the following day, and Tom and I were left to go on with our fishing operations. Tom had never done any such work before, but he was teachable and diligent, and proved a splendid companion.

All this time, however, I was in perfect misery with one of my teeth. It had been aching for over two months, and had taken the pleasure out of all my later trips. Whether hunting the Stoneys, chasing buffalo, or at home at Victoria, that old tooth kept on the jump and made life miserable. I had burned it with a red-hot iron, had poulticed it, had done everything I could; but as there was not a pair of forceps in the country I could not have it pulled. Now the overhauling of nets morning and night and the working in the cold water was making my tooth worse than ever. Sometimes I was almost distracted with the gnawing ache and pain.

After putting in a terrible night, I said to Tom, "Are you willing to stay here alone while I go to the mission and see if I cannot in some way obtain relief from this tooth?" The plucky fellow said, "Go ahead, John, and I will do the best I can until you send some one to help me."

So, away I ran, with only a light coat on and but a small piece of dried meat stuck into my bosom. In ordinary times the forty miles would have been but a little run. Now it seemed a fearful distance. I fairly dragged my legs along, and was almost thoroughly played out when at last, late in the evening, I reached the mission. Father was away at Edmonton.

When Father came home, Peter, who was with him, went right on to the fishing to take my place. Father got a pair of pinchers and with the aid of Larsen, the carpenter, filed them into the shape of forceps. With this improvised instrument he set to work to extract the tooth. After five fruitless efforts at this, he broke the tooth off square with the gums. Now it ached worse than ever!

Winter had set in, and the river soon was frozen over so as to admit of travel. Mr. Woolsey having business at Edmonton, I took him with cariole and dogs, following the ice all the way there and back. That tooth kept up its aching, more or less, all the time until we came within thirty miles of home. The last day of the trip, while we were having lunch, I was eating a piece of pemmican, when all of a sudden my tooth stopped aching. I felt a hole in it, and also felt something queer in my mouth. Taking this out, I found it to be a piece of the nerve.

The pain was gone, and my relief may be imagined. I think I must have gained about ten pounds in weight within the next two weeks. Nine years later, when paying my first visit to Ontario, I sat down in cold blood and told the dentist to dig out those roots. Verily, there was deep-rooted in me the desire for revenge on that tooth. He did dig it out, and I was pleased and satisfied to part with my old enemy.

With the first approach of winter, the majority of the Indians recrossed the Saskatchewan and pitched southward for buffalo. Some waited until the ice-bridge was formed, and a few went northward into the woods to trap and hunt for fur. Even so, it rarely happened that there were no Indians about the place. Strangers would come out of their way to camp for a day or two beside the new mission. They had heard that missionaries were settling on the river near the "Hairy Bag," which was the old name given to the valley just back of the mission house as it had been a favourite feeding ground for the buffalo. The visitors wanted to see for themselves what was going on and what was the purpose of such effort.

Because the missionary became noted as a "medicine man," able to help the diseased, many were brought from afar that they might reap the benefit of his care. Then all the hungry and naked hunters, those out of luck, upon whom some spell had been cast (as they believed) so that their nets failed to catch, their guns missed fire, and their traps snapped, or their dead-falls fell without trapping anything—where else should these unfortunates go for help and advice and comfort but to the "praying man." And thus with our large party, and the very many other calls upon our commissariat, it kept some of us on the jump to gather provisions sufficient to "keep the pot boiling."

Already, because of the snow coming earlier, we had hauled most of our fish from the lake, fairly rushing things after we had the road broken. Generally two trips were made in three days, and now and then a trip a day. Away at two or three o'clock in the morning, forty miles out light; then, lashing a hundred or more frozen whitefish on our narrow dog sled, home again the same evening with the load, yoked to hardy dogs and still hardier men. One such trip was enough for any weakling or faint-heart who might try it.

Owing to the great demands on our larder, we found our supply of fresh meat nearly exhausted, and so decided to go out in search of a fresh supply. There was a good foot of snow on the ground around Victoria and more to the south and east where the Indians and buffalo were, but this did not stop us from starting out. The party consisted of Father, Peter, Tom, a man named Johnson, and myself. We took both horses and dogs. The second day out we encountered intensely cold weather, and this decided us to strike eastward into the hills along the south of the chain of lakes.

The third day we killed two bulls, and as the meat was very good, Father told Tom and me to load our sleds and return to the mission, and then to come right back again. Off we started with our loads, but as we had a road to break across country our progress was slow. We had no snowshoes. I had to wade ahead of the dogs while Tom brought up the rear.

That night was one of the coldest in my experience, and I know what cold means if any man does. Tom and I each had a small blanket. We made as good a camp as we could by clearing away the snow and putting down a lot of frozen willows. We kept up a good fire, but the heat did not seem to have any radiating power that night. An almost infinite wall of frosty atmosphere was pressing in on us from all sides. Putting our unlined capotes beneath and the two blankets over us, we tried to sleep, for we had travelled steadily and worked hard all the day.

I went to sleep. Tom shivered beside me. Presently he woke me up by exclaiming, "John, for God's sake make a fire! I am freezing!" I hurried as fast as I could, and soon had a big blaze going. Then I got Tom up and held him close over the fire, rubbing and chafing, and turning him all the while, until the poor fellow was somewhat restored. We did not try to sleep any more that night, but busied ourselves in chopping and carrying logs for our fire.

With the first glimmer of day we were away, and steadily kept our weary wading through the deep, loose snow. About eight in the evening we came out on the trail leading to the mission. We would have been home by midnight, only I had to make another fire about ten o'clock and give Tom another thawing out. He was a slight slim fellow and the bitter cold seemed to go right through him; but he was a lad of real grit and true pluck. Fortunately for Tom and me, it was between two and three o'clock in the morning when we reached the mission. This gave us the day's rest; otherwise we would have felt duty bound to turn right about and go back to our party.

A little after midnight Tom and I set forth on our return. The cold was intense, but we were light, and running and riding we made a tremendous day of it, coming about noon to where we had parted from our friends. Following them up, we came to where they had found the trail of an Indian camp and gone on it. We camped when night came. As we had now a distinct trail, we left our camp in the night and a little after daylight had the satisfaction of seeing the white smoke from many lodges rising high into the cold, clear air in the distance. This stimulated us, and within two hours we were in the camp and again with our friends. They had fallen in with a party of Indians from Whitefish Lake and north of it, and Father and party were now in Chief Child's lodge.

They had secured fine loads of fresh and dried meats and were ready to start back when we reached the camp. So, we packed up and headed for home. As we could travel faster with the dog trains, and make longer distances than the horses, Peter and Tom and I went on, leaving Father and Johnson to come as they could. We were home and had made another trip to the fishery and back by the time they got in with their loads.

Now Mr. Woolsey was ready to set out on the missionary tour to Edmonton, usually taken during the holidays. He planned to reach that place the day before Christmas. I drove the cariole. We had with us a newcomer, one "Billy" Smith, a man whom we had known at Norway House and who had drifted into this upper country. Billy drove the baggage and "grub train." At the same time as we started, Father and Peter and the others set out to procure another load of meat, for there was no telling where the buffalo might be driven to in a short time.

We reached the Fort on the twenty-fourth, remained there during the holiday week, and started back the day after New Year's.

While we were there a small party of Mountain Stoneys came in to trade. With these was Jonas, one of Rundle's converts. He understood Cree well. Mr. Woolsey arranged with him to return with us to Victoria, as Father and he were very desirous of securing the translation of some hymns into Stoney. Jonas brought a companion with him. Just as we were starting from Edmonton, Billy Smith was bitten in the hand by one of the dogs. The wound became very bad almost immediately and grew worse as we neared home.

Billy Smith had a terrible time with his hand. Inflammation set in, mortification threatened, and some of our party had to work day and night to save him.

Jonas and his companion came into the mission some hours after us. For several days Peter and Jonas worked on the translation of some hymns into the Stoney language. Then Jonas, with such help as Father and Mr. Woolsey could give him, and with a copy of these hymns in the syllabic characters in his bosom, set out on his three-hundred-mile tramp to his mountain home.

The rest of his small party who had visited Edmonton were attacked by the Blackfeet when about fifty miles south of the Fort. Several were killed and wounded on both sides. The Stoneys, though much outnumbered, eventually succeeded in driving their enemies away. It may be said that Jonas saved his life that time by coming with our company to Victoria. Fortunately he missed any such mishap on his way home and reached his people in good time. He was able to teach others these Gospel hymns for which he had travelled so far in the intense cold of a Northern winter.

During this winter of 1863-64 a camp of about forty lodges of Wood Stoneys came to the mission from the north. After staying with us for a couple of days, they pitched across to hunt for buffalo for a while. These people frequented the wooded country to the north of the Saskatchewan, and were known as "wood hunters." Moose and elk, deer and bear, and all manner of fur-bearing animals in this country were their legitimate prey, but occasionally they made a raid on the buffalo. They were great gamblers and polygamists, and generally a pretty wild lot. They spoke the same language as the Mountain Stoneys, with some shades of difference, mostly dialectical. These people had been gone about a month across into the buffalo country when they sent us word to come for provisions.

We went, and found them in a thicket of timber, among rolling hills near Birch Lake, southeast of the mission about seventy-five miles. From them we secured four splendid loads of dried provisions and grease; but we had a time of it in getting out of those hills with our heavily loaded sleds.

On one of our trips, some time in January, I became acquainted with a gentleman named "The Muddy Bull." When I say "gentleman," I mean it in its literal sense. He was one of "nature's noblemen." We made arrangements with him to become our hunter. While we were hauling in meat, he and his family followed the buffalo and he killed and hauled in and staged near his camp. We lost no time in securing the meat and very soon had a fine pile in our storehouse. While we were hauling in we made his lodge our home.

His wife was a natural lady. Later on, Father had the pleasure of marrying them and of baptizing and receiving them into the Church. The question which often puzzled me was: "When were they converted?" For, it always seemed as if they were already converted when I first met them. Noah and Barbara became their Christian names.

"Muddy Bull" was a splendid hunter. He had made a study of the instincts of the animals within his range. Soon after the time of our first meeting he killed seven buffaloes within fifty feet square of ground, and that with an old pot-metal flint-lock gun, muzzle-loading and single-barrelled at that. I have seen him with the same gun, and with his horse at full gallop over a rough country, knock three buffaloes down, one after the other, almost as fast as an ordinary hunter would with a Winchester. The quality of the animals spoke the true hunter. Many men could kill, but not many could pick as "Muddy Bull" could. No wonder that having found him we retained him as our hunter for several years.

During the winter Peter and I made a short trip with dog teams across the White Mud River in search of the white clay from which the river took its name. This clay was useful in whitening chimneys and walls, and made even a log house look far more respectable. We found the clay deposit, and then as we tracked buffalo going northward, we concluded to camp and have a hunt.

Tying up our dogs, we started out on snowshoes, each taking a different direction. The snow was very deep. In the woods it was heavy, but on the plains where it was better packed one could make much faster time.

Presently I heard a shot, and going to where the sound came from, I saw Peter standing at a little distance from a huge bull. The animal evidently was badly hit and had settled himself into a bed in the deep snow. I went over to where Peter stood and, taking my snowshoes off, stuck them into the snow. Then I walked towards the head of the bull. He was a magnificent animal, with fine horns, long shaggy beard, and very black woolly mane and neck.

Suddenly, without a moment's warning, he sprang at me — sprang something like the clay pigeon does when the trap is pulled. I bounded from before him for my life. Down the slope, across a valley, up the opposite hill, I flew. Nor did I even look back until I stood on the summit of the knoll. Then I saw the bull going back and again settling himself in the same snowy bed. Gathering up my courage, I approached him more cautiously and shot him in the head, killing him instantly. When I saw my flying tracks in the snow I could hardly believe that I had made such leaps and bounds. Peter said he "never saw anything like it," and probably he never had.

For some time we had two men sawing out lumber at the old place beyond Smoking Lake, and at intervals we made flying trips out there for this lumber. For instance, if we reached home on Friday night, instead of starting back on Saturday to the plains, we would go out to the lumber shanty, thirty-five miles distant, and loading up, reach home with our loads of lumber the same evening. This would give us Sunday at home, which, though not happening often, was always a delight. Now, as the spring was drawing on, and the snow beginning to melt, we rushed this lumber out.

Besides the lumber we took out a large number of tamarack logs to make a strong, high picket around the mission house. From our experience in the fall when the large camps came in around us, Father considered this prudent. Also, the Indians to the south, the hereditary enemies of those we were among, would very soon know — if they did not now know — of our settlement. Already stolen horses and scalps had been brought into the camp beside the mission, and it would follow inevitably that the avenger would come along later. A large, strong palisade would command respect from the lawless around home, and be a great help from enemies who might come from a distance.

In the meantime, Larsen and Father, and in fact everybody who had an odd hour to spare, had gone on with the work of the mission house. As we had no stoves, it was thought necessary to build two immense chimneys in the house, one at each end. This took time and heavy labour. Then the drying and dressing of the lumber for floors and ceilings and partitions was tedious work, as anyone knows who ever had anything to do with "whip-sawed" lumber. You could hardly give away such boards in the days of sawmills and planing machines, but our party had to straighten and plane and groove and tongue and bead, all by hand, and out of very poor material.

All were looking forward to the finishing of the new house, and none more than my mother. For seven months she had been

obliged to put up with the crowded conditions of our comparatively small one-roomed log building. Thirteen of us called it
home, ate there when we were at the mission, and nearly all slept
there. All the cooking, washing, and other household work was
done in this little place. Then strangers would come in for a night
as they travelled to and fro. True, there were not many of these,
and their coming was a welcome change, even if the house did
become more crowded. Indians, too, would visit the missionary,
and they must be welcomed to his home, or they would go away
with a very low estimate of the faith he came to propagate. Of
course the brunt of the discomfort fell upon Mother. No wonder
she was looking ardently for the finishing of the new home.

Our last trip of the season by dog sled was to bring some seed
potatoes from Whitefish Lake. We had deferred this on account
of frost, but now were caught by heat. The snow melted before
we were half-way home, and we had to take poles and push
behind those loads for long, weary miles before we struck the
river, when we had the ice for the rest of the way home. Peter,
Tom, and I brought about twenty bushels between us. By the
time we got them to Victoria those potatoes were worth a great
deal, for they had cost us many a push and tug and pull to get
them through sound and safe.

FOURTEEN

To Fort Garry

Early in April I took Mr. Woolsey and my sister Georgina to Edmonton. Mr. Woolsey expected to return east during the summer, and was to make his farewell visit. My sister was invited by the Chief Factor's lady, Mrs. Christie, to spend some time with her. We travelled on horseback with pack-horses. We were three days on the trip up, and I was two coming home, after safely delivering my passengers at Edmonton.

Soon after I came back Father startled me by saying he wanted me to go to Fort Garry to bring out the supplies for the Whitefish Lake and Victoria missions. He said that the Hudson's Bay Company had notified all missionaries that their transport was needed for their own business, and suggested that the missionaries make their own arrangements for obtaining supplies. Therefore he wanted me to go down and purchase and bring up what was needed for the Methodist missions on the Saskatchewan. I was to take horses and men from both missions, and also purchase some cattle down there to bring up for work and for dairy purposes. Thus I found my work cut out for me for several months ahead, and I immediately started making preparations.

The Indians had now begun to arrive in large bands, and very soon our valley was full of life. Men, both wild and partly civilized, surrounded the place. A large number of the former had passed by, seeking scalps and horses. They would be drifting in later on.

Already that spring there had been a big fight between a party from our camp and the Blackfeet. The Crees were surrounded and kept for two nights and nearly two days in the pits they had dug with their knives. The Blackfeet were ten times their number, and kept them well under cover, but did not muster courage sufficient to rush in, or the Crees would have been cleaned out in short order. As it was, several were killed. Of two I knew, one was killed and the other shot in the breast, but recovered as by a miracle.

Father and Peter would now be on a continuous strain of work for the next six weeks — planting, hoeing, teaching, preaching, healing, counselling, civilizing, and Christianizing. Night and day, constant watchfulness and care would be required. A very little thing might make a very big row. Life and death were in the balance, and the missionary had to be a man of fine tact and quick judgement as well as a man of prayer. The turbulent element was sometimes in the majority, for large numbers of Plains Crees had come in with the quieter Wood Indians. Saucy, proud, arrogant, lawless fellows they were, every one of them. Yet, they were courteous and kind if one only took them the right way. And to be able to do this, we were studying all the time.

Mother and my young sisters moved in and out among these painted and war-bedizened crowds, all unconscious of their danger, and it was well it was so. But Father and myself, and others also, felt the strain of possible tragedy. Maskepetoon when at the mission was a tower of strength and a great source of comfort. Even in his own camp there were a number of jealous factions, and born chief that he was, he often found them very hard to control. This was the first attempt by any Church to establish a mission among these people, and under such circumstances we put our trust in God — but we kept our powder dry.

It was with an anxious yet sanguine mind that during the last days of April, 1864, I left parents and mission party behind and started eastward for Fort Garry. I had with me a French half-breed, Baptiste by name, and we were to be joined by the men and horses from Mr. Steinhauer's mission some fifty or sixty miles farther east. We had a pack-horse to carry our food and bedding, and were in the saddle ourselves — that is, we had two Indian pads, as the Mexican saddle had not yet made its appearance so far north.

The second day we were joined by our comrades from Whitefish Lake, my friend Ka-kake being one of the number. They had a cart with them. Our party now was complete, and consisted of five men and fifteen horses. As it was early in the season, and our horses had come through a pretty hard winter with considerable work and consequently were somewhat run down, we travelled slowly, averaging about thirty miles per day. Our provision was pemmican, but we supplemented this as we travelled with ducks, geese, and chickens. Yet many a meal was hard grease pemmican straight.

We travelled only the six days, faithfully and rigidly observing the Sabbath. We had prayer morning and night, my men taking turn in conducting worship. On Sunday we rested and sang a number of hymns, and as we were speaking Cree all the time, I was constantly improving myself in the language, and learning the idioms and traditions of the people.

We passed Fort Pitt and came to Jackfish Lake. Here we found the camp of Salteaux that frequented this lake. They were feasting on the carcasses of a great herd of buffalo that had been drowned in the lake the previous winter. Too many had got together in some stampede across the ice and had broken through. Now that the ice was off the lake, the carcasses were drifting ashore. These improvident people were glad to get the meat. They offered us some, and though Ka-kake took it out of deference to their kindness, he watched his opportunity and threw it away.

Some of the younger men came to our camp that night. Ka-

kake, who was a sort of kinsman of theirs, tried to show them the folly of some lawless acts blamed on them. (These fellows had a hard name.) One of them began to speak quite excitedly: "You seem to make much ado about our taking some plunder and demanding tribute of parties passing through our country. What will you think when we really do something? For, we are disposed to organize and take these Hudson's Bay forts, and drive all the white men out of this country. Then you will have something to talk about!"

Just here I thought it was my turn to join in the conversation, and quietly snatching a handful of blades of grass, I picked the shortest and smallest one of these and held it in my other hand. Then looking at the excited Indian, I said, "My friend, I have listened to you. Now listen to me. Look at this handful of grass in my hand. These are many and big and strong, and this little one in my other hand is small and weak and alone. This little weak, lone grass represents the white man as he now is in this country. There are a few traders and a few missionaries, but they are as this little grass in strength and number, as you look at them.

"But if you hurt them in any way, as you say you will, this bunch of many and strong grasses I hold in my hand represents the multitude your own conduct would bring into this country to avenge them. You say you can easily wipe out the white men now in this country. Have you thought that they have the guns and the ammunition and the real strength? Can you or any of your people make guns or ammunition? Why talk so foolishly and thoughtlessly?"

All of this Ka-kake strongly corroborated. When the Salteaux went away he turned to me and thanked me for the way I had spoken to that man and his party. "It will do them good; they will think about it," he said. At the same time we tethered our horses and guarded them well.

We crossed the North Saskatchewan at Carlton, passed Duck Lake, and crossed the south branch of the river where Batoche settled some years later. The next day we killed several antelope and ate them up in what seemed to me no time at all. Then we rode over the alkali plains and journeyed through the Touchwood Hills, where we shot a great big bear. Thus antelope steak and bear's ribs, with fowl occasionally, and eggs of more or less ancient date now and then, varied the monotony of the ever-lasting pemmican.

We traversed Pheasant Plains and Cut Arm Creek and camped at evening on the high bank of the Qu'Appelle River, beside a spring. The next afternoon Ka-kake and I, leaving our companions to cross the Assiniboine above the mouth of the Qu'Appelle, detoured by way of Fort Ellice. Mrs. MacKay, the wife of the gentleman in charge of the Fort, very kindly invited me to have supper with them. What should be on the table but pancakes and maple syrup! I had not tasted maple syrup for four years, had not had a slice of bread for two years, had not even tasted anything cooked from flour for some time. These were things I had been accustomed to, almost bred on, all my life before coming to the North-West.

We rejoined our companions at Bird Tail Creek, camping on the spot where now the town of Birtle stands. This was Saturday night, and during that Sunday camp on the bank of Bird Tail Creek, I had my first and only difference with Ka-kake. Some hunters on the way out by Fort Ellice camped beside us, and from these Ka-kake learned that friends of his were camped about twenty miles farther on. About the middle of the afternoon, he and the two Indians from Whitefish Lake began to catch their horses and make as if they were going to start. I asked what they meant, and Ka-kake told me that they were going on and would wait for us in the morning. I said he might go on if he chose, but I would not consent to his taking the horses belonging to Mr. Steinhauer, as these were in my charge, and I did not intend to have them travel on Sunday. He was firm, but I was firmer. Finally Ka-kake turned the horses loose and gave it up. I believed I was right at the time, and therefore I acted as I did.

The next day Baptiste and I went ahead. I wanted to get through my business as quickly as possible and give more time to the homeward trip, when we would have heavy loads.

The first night we camped with a large party of plain hunters, on their way out for a summer hunt. These men were from all over the Red River settlement, from the White Horse plains, and Portage la Prairie. Their encampment was like a good-sized village. They must have had five hundred or more carts, besides many waggons. This number would be very much augmented from Fort Ellice and other points.

Two such parties went out on the plains after buffalo every summer for the purpose of making dried provisions. Some of these would also make fall and winter forays for fresh meat. These were the men who owned the rich portions of Manitoba, the Portage plains, and the banks of the Assiniboine and Red Rivers. But what cared they for rich homesteads so long as buffalo could be found within five or six hundred miles? These owners of the best wheat fields in the world were willing to take their chance of a very risky mode of life because they came of a hunting breed. Environment stamps itself deep upon the race.

We jogged along, Baptiste and I, across the Little Saskatchewan, and by the two crossings of the White Mud, and coming to the third crossing in the evening, found a Church of England mission with the Rev. Mr. George in charge. Mrs. George was very kind, and for the first time in two years I had a square meal of bread and butter. I had to fairly curb my appetite.

Next morning Mrs. George gave us a fresh loaf of bread and some butter for our lunch that day. We had not gone a mile from her hospitable home when I said, "Baptiste, don't you think we could carry that bread and butter somewhere else very much better than on that pack-horse?"

"Oh, yes, Mr. John," was his answer.

We thereupon alighted, took the tempting loaf from the pack, ate it with eager relish, and then went on quite satisfied.

We rode through the Portage, finding at that time but two white men settled there. As I had a letter for Archdeacon Cochrane, we called for a few minutes on that venerable prelate. I found him quite an old man. That day he seemed somewhat discouraged, for he asked me if I did not think the mixed bloods among whom he was labouring must first be civilized before they could be Christianized. I ventured to say that I thought Christianity was the main factor in real civilization. Then he asked me what my opinion was of the war in the States, and I told him that I knew very little about it. He said he was in sympathy with the South. At this I was astonished but did not venture to say anything, for he was an old man, and I was but a boy.

As I rode away I wondered how a gentleman of his age and experience and education and calling could hold such views as to be in sympathy with rebellion and slavery. There must be something in this I do not understand, thought I. But if there was any good reason for such a position I have never yet come across it.

That night we camped with Peter's brother-in-law who lived at the High Bluff. He received us kindly. The next day we jogged along the north bank of the Assiniboine, around the Big Bend, and through the White Horse Plains.

As we were passing a house Baptiste said, "Mr. John, my friends used to live here. Stop a minute and let me see." So, we approached the house and found that the woman of this place was Baptiste's cousin, and though many years had elapsed since they had met, the recognition was mutual and joyous. As the day was extremely warm, this woman offered us some nice cold milk. I drank sparingly, but my man Baptiste indulged in it recklessly.

Mounting our horses, we resumed the chronic jog and had not gone many miles when I heard a groan. Looking back I saw Baptiste with his hand pressing his stomach and seeming woefully dismal.

"What is the matter?" I enquired.

"Oh! Mr. John, I am so sore."

"You deserve to be. You should not have drunk so much milk," said I.

In the evening we came to the farm of Mr. Gowler. I had letters for him from both Father and Mr. Woolsey, and I hoped to make his home my headquarters while doing my business and gathering my stock and loads for the West. Riding into the yard, we found the old farmer had just finished churning and was enjoying a bowl of fresh buttermilk. He kindly offered me some. I declined with thanks, but said my man was very fond of milk. At once Mr. Gowler gave Baptiste a big bowl of buttermilk. His code of etiquette would not allow him to decline, and though in misery already he drank it. Like many another simple person, he was the slave of social rule.

Mr. Gowler had come out in the Hudson's Bay Company's service, by way of Hudson Bay. Eventually he had gone free and settled on the Assiniboine a few miles west of Fort Garry. At this time he had the largest farm in the Red River settlement. He had been an English Wesleyan Methodist in the old country, and though he had allied himself to the Anglican Church when he came out here, yet he retained a warm feeling toward those of his early persuasion. Thus Mr. Woolsey and Father had met him. Thus I had come to him to arrange for a camp, a pasture, and a home while in the settlement. To all of these he made me heartily welcome.

I had no trouble about the year's supplies for the missions, as they had all been requisitioned early in the year. My business was the arranging of transport. I must obtain carts and harness and oxen. As the several plains-hunting parties had recently started out, I had some difficulty in finding enough for my needs. But after a few days' shopping around, I secured all I wanted. For my oxen, fine big fellows, I paid on an average seven pounds or about thirty-five dollars apiece.

I purchased four quiet milch cows, for which I paid from fifteen to eighteen dollars each, thinking as I bought them how much they would be welcomed by our people at yonder mission. I also bought ten sacks of flour, paying one pound twelve per sack of ninety-six pounds, and two shillings for the sack. Add to this the freight to Victoria, and the first cost there of each sack would be $18.50. I gave five sacks to each mission and allowed a sack for the men of each party *en route*.

I bought, too, a promising colt, descendant of Fire Away, a very famous horse the Hudson's Bay Company had imported from the old country. For this three-year-old colt I paid fourteen pounds, or seventy dollars of our money. In making my purchases I handled the first "Hudson's Bay blankets" I had ever seen. These were large five-shilling and five-pound notes issued by the Company, and which I drew from them on Father's order.

In the course of my business I was in Old Fort Garry a number of times. I saw St. Boniface, then a very small place just across the river, and the home of Bishop Taché. I was in and out of the five or six houses which then formed the nucleus of the little village called Winnipeg. I rode frequently through the parish of St. John's, passing the house of Bishop Anderson, the Anglican head of Rupert's Land. I went down into Kildonan and spent a night in the home of the Rev. Dr. Black, who was one of Father's dear friends. I also met there the Rev. Mr. Nisbet, who later on founded the mission work at Prince Albert.

I visited some of the original Scotch settlers and was looked upon by the elders as a degenerate because, as they expressed it, "She couldna spoket the Gaelic." I spent two Sundays in this settlement, hearing Dr. Black the first Sunday. The next Sabbath I worshipped with the Anglicans and heard the Rev. Henry Cochrane preach an eloquent and inspiring sermon, and was glad that a genuine native had reached such a position.

My man Baptiste had disappeared, forgetting his wife and children on the Saskatchewan. His old associates and whiskey were too much for him. I could not give the time to looking for him, but hired instead one of Mr. Gowler's sons, Oliver by name. As I was still short of help, I was very glad that I came across a gentleman by the name of Connor and his son, a young man about my age, who were desirous of making the trip to the Saskatchewan. As they had but one cart between them, I secured the son to drive carts for me. My party was also joined by a Scotchman who was desirous of crossing the mountains to British Columbia. He also had but one cart.

Because the Whitefish Lake party had horses pulling their carts and would travel faster than we could, especially in hot weather, I let them go on ahead of us. Our party was composed of Mr. Connor and the Scotchman, my two men, and myself—five in all.

FIFTEEN

Waggons Home

It was about the last of June or the first of July that we rolled out of Mr. Gowler's farmyard on the trail leading across the plains. The first day or two we had considerable trouble with our cattle. One cow was determined to go back, so I caught her and tied her behind a cart drawn by a ponderous ox. She rebelled at this and threw herself down, but the ox kept on as if the weight dragging behind was a small matter. When we came to a shallow creek in which there were some sharp stones on the bottom, the cow was dragged over them. She jumped to her feet and after that led on as we wished.

Very soon all broke in to the routine of the journey in good shape, and we had very little trouble after the first week with any of our loose stock. Let one of those ironless carts squeak, and the cows were up and alongside with all the alacrity of a soldier answering the bugle note.

There had been considerable rain, and for the first three weeks after we started it rained very heavily at times. As there was not a tent in the party, we each got under a cart, and while the rain came perpendicularly we were passably dry; but the mosquitoes were sometimes awfully annoying. The rains made the roads very heavy in places, but we came along as far as the second crossing of the White Mud without having to move loads. Here we were forced to raft everything, which means a great amount of labour and also a long delay. I made a raft of cartwheels, and pulling this to and fro with ropes, we ferried our goods and chattels over.

Having let the Indians go on, my party as now constituted was altogether tenderfoot in its make-up, though my two years on the Saskatchewan had modified my status somewhat. As it was, I had all the planning and also a large portion of the work to do. To unload your carts and make your rafts, and ferry over piecemeal your loads and harness and cart-boxes and whole travelling outfit; to watch your stock in the meantime, and that closely, or else lose hours or even days in hunting for them; to keep your stuff from the wet from above as well as beneath, and in doing so get more or less wet yourself; to make smudges to save your cattle and horses from being eaten alive by mosquitoes and the prairie black flies called "bulldogs"; to fight these exceedingly energetic denizens of the air while you are trying to work — if you can imagine all this, you will have an idea of summer transport across bridgeless and ferryless streams in a new country.

Having passed the second, we went on to the third crossing of the White Mud, and like the man with the two daughters whom he called Kate and Duplicate, we simply duplicated the last crossing here, only that it was "the same and more of it." The creeks had been very small on our way down, but now seeing them so full after the heavy rains, and giving us so much trouble to cross, I began to apprehend some difficulty at the Little Saskatchewan, for this was a river and rapid at that.

However, we stopped short of this one morning for breakfast, and while the boys were making a fire I walked on to the river and was delighted to note that, while it was muddy and swift, it was still fordable. This I knew without trying, as I had taken its measure on my way down.

Just then, as I stood for a moment on its bank before returning to my camp, two travellers on horseback, with a pack-horse, came down the hill on the other side. They looked at the stream and at once pronounced it unfordable. Then, without stopping to ask me, they got off their horses, unsaddled and unpacked, took out their axe and went for some timber to make a raft. I thought I would have some fun with them, so I waited until they had carried up some logs for the raft. Then as they stood on the bank resting for a little, I walked down into the stream and across to them. As I had estimated at first glance, there was no more than twenty or twenty-four inches of water.

These travellers looked astonished and seemed indignant that I had not told them. "Why did you not tell us the river was fordable?" said one.

"Why did you not ask me?" I answered.

Then one blamed the other who was acting as guide, and told him he ought to have known better than to let them make such fools of themselves. Here I spoke up and said, "Well, as it is fordable, you had better saddle up and come across and have some breakfast with us."

Fording the Little Saskatchewan, we continued our journey. One day we stopped at noon on the shore of Shoal Lake, and here while our stock were resting I made an experiment. We had brought with us from the mission a fine strong mare about seven years of age which had never been broken either to drive or to ride. She was very wild. She would follow the carts and stay with our horses, that was all.

My plan was to take her out into the lake and break her there. We made a corral with the carts. I lassoed the mare, and haltering her, stripped off my clothes and swam out into the lake with her. Then I quietly slipped on her back. She gave a plunge or two, but only succeeded in ducking herself and then settled down to straight swimming. After a while I headed her for the shore. As soon as she got squarely on the bottom she began to buck, so I headed her out again into the lake. Presently I could take her out on the beach and canter up and down as nicely as with an old saddle-horse. Then I dressed, and putting a saddle-pad on, rode her all the afternoon.

Rolling on as well as we could, heeding but little the mud and mosquitoes and pelting rains, in good time we reached the Assiniboine. We were two days rafting that stream and the large part of another in doubling and portaging up the big sand hill which forms the north bank of the Assiniboine at this point.

Leaving my party in camp on the bank of the Qu'Appelle, I forded this stream and rode over to Fort Ellice. I hoped to secure some dried meat or pemmican, as we were living now entirely on flour and milk, and I wanted to use the flour as little as possible. Mrs. MacKay said that there were no provisions at the Fort, but that she expected soon to hear from her husband who had gone on to the plains. Fortunately for me, while we were talking a party drove into the Fort with several cart-loads of provisions, and thus I secured both pemmican and dried meat.

Steadily we pushed our way westward — some days, when cool and cloudy, making good time; then, when it was hot, going more leisurely. Travelling early and late, we would keep at the long trail. Then an axle would break and this would bring us up standing. Sometimes a dowel-pin snapped, or a felloe split, and mending and lashing still, we rolled toward the setting sun.

There is no better place than around the campfire, and on a trip like ours, to size up men and display one's own idiosyncrasies. Mr. Connor, the gentleman who had joined me at the Red River, proved to be a very good companion. He had travelled and read and was in the early forties a minister of the Methodist Church. Owing to some misunderstanding he had given up the ministry and gone afloat — and was still floating. He was generally bright and cheerful and helpful. Sometimes he fell into a streak of melancholy; however, that darkened his own day more than anyone else's. He drives his own cart. This he has shingled with pieces of tarred bale covers and at night sleeps in it. His yoke of steers, though at first somewhat balky in mudholes, after I have drilled them a few times and got them to recognize my voice in a real western yell, come along all right.

His son James, who is one of my men, is a short, sturdy fellow. Being strong and hearty, he is fast adapting himself to this new life. My other man, Oliver, is but an overgrown boy. He has had very little opportunity in life, no chance at school, and is rather simple-minded, but willing and strong.

The Scotchman, who is on his way across the mountains, walks by his own cart and horse most of the day's march. He is "canny and careful" about the camp. For the most part he is silent and reserved, but in a pinch, and at river crossings, he lends a strong hand.

We had three dogs with us, one belonging to the Scotchman and the others to me. Both of mine were a present from a clergyman I met in the settlement, one a duck dog and the other a small rat terrier. The latter supported the two former on the road by killing gophers for them. This little fellow was extremely agile. He would jump up on my foot in the stirrup, and at the next leap be in the saddle beside me. There he would rest for a little while, perhaps until the next gopher popped in sight, when with a bound he would be away. This he would keep up the whole day long. At night I might wrap my blanket as tightly as I pleased about me, but the little scamp would crawl in somehow and sleep beside me.

One day when we were hunting moulting ducks during our noon spell, he got after a big stock duck and took hold of the bird's tail-feathers. The duck made for the lake with the dog in tow. The little fellow was gritty and held on while the bird pulled him far out into the lake. It was amusing to see the small dog being whirled along by the duck, who was flapping his featherless wings and swimming at a great rate. Presently the dog, wanting to bark, opened his mouth. The duck dove under immediately it was loose. My little pet swam ashore.

On a Saturday evening we camped in the Touchwood Hills and found ourselves near a solitary lodge occupied by an old Indian and his aged wife. The *mesa-koo-tom* or service berry were very plentiful all through the hills, and this old couple had gathered and dried a large quantity. I was glad to trade a bag of these from them to take home to our people, for any kind of dried fruit had been a scarce article with us. On Sunday two boys came in from the plains with a horse-load of dried provisions. They were the old man's grandchildren and had come for the old folks. The boys said the buffalo were about fifty miles south of us. Monday morning I traded some dried provisions from the old man and we parted company.

Four days later we camped in a small round prairie, backed by a range of hills and fringed around by willow and poplar brush. We had pulled our carts into a line, with our campfire in the centre. We were sufficiently north, as we thought, to be comparatively safe from horse-thieves and war parties, so we merely hobbled our horses. Making a good smudge near our own fire, we rolled in our blankets, each man under a cart, except Mr. Connor, who slept in his.

Some time in the night I was awakened by my little dog, who had crept under my blanket as usual, and now startled me by springing forth and barking vigorously. As I raised myself on my elbow, I saw that the two larger dogs were charging at something quite near.

The moon was about three parts full, and the night quiet and almost clear. From under the shadow of the cart I could see our horses feeding near the smoke. Presently I discovered an object crawling up to come between the carts and the horses. At first I thought it was a big grey wolf; but as the dogs rushed at it, I saw that it did not recede, but came on.

I reached for my gun and watched closely, and presently saw the object pick up a stick and throw it at the dogs. This convinced me that it was someone trying to steal our horses. His aim evidently was to creep in between us and our stock, and after gently driving them away, he would then cut the hobbles and run them off.

Having made sure that what I saw was a human being, and a would-be horse-thief — or worse — I immediately planned to intercept him. So I in turn began to crawl along the shade of the carts until I was under the last one, which was Mr. Connor's. Here I waited and watched until, seeing the fellow repeatedly frighten the dogs away, I was sure it was a man. He was slowly coming up on hands and knees; when he was near the first horse, I took deliberate aim and fired at him. My gun was loaded with shot, and fortunately for him was only a single barrel, or I would have given him the other. I was not at that moment in a mood to spare a horse-thief. My shot at once knocked him flat.

When the smoke had cleared away I saw him starting to crawl off. I jumped for him. He rose to his feet and ran for all he was worth towards the nearest brush. I dropped my gun and picked up a pole that lay in my way and was overtaking him fast when he reached the thicket. Then, thinking he might not be alone, I ran back for my gun. My companions by this time were all up, so we made ready for an attack. Tying up our horses, we watched and guarded until daylight, but were not further molested.

By now I concluded that the thief was alone, and I became very anxious about him. I knew I had hit him, but to what extent I did not know. Taking a man with me, we went on his track and found that he had lost considerable blood, had rested and, we supposed, had in some way bound up his wound and then gone on. As we tracked him I concluded by his step that he was but slightly hurt and would reach his camp all right. This relieved my mind considerably, but it was not until the next year we heard about the fellow. Then it came out that I blew the top off the man's shoulder, and after a hard journey back to camp, he lay some three months before recovering.

I have always felt thankful I did not kill the fellow, but most certainly I wanted to at the time. If my gun had been loaded with ball, or that bit of prairie had been longer — for I was coming up on him fast and the pole I carried was a strong one — the results might have been different.

We were now approaching the south branch of the Saskatchewan. The streams we had crossed so far were as child's play compared to this. I galloped ahead to the river and saw it was booming. I rode down the several hills to the river's brink and felt almost sick at heart when I found there was no boat in sight. However, at the top of the hill I now noticed a pole stuck in the ground and something white at the end of it. Galloping over,

I found a note tied to the pole which said, "Down in the woods in the direction this stick points, there is a skin canoe."

The note also said, "In the bow of the canoe you will find a chunk of hard grease." This was to pitch its seams and make it waterproof.

I found the canoe placed high on the limbs of some trees to keep it from the wolves, who would soon gnaw its skin covering. I saw it was very small, being made of two buffalo cowhides stretched over a frame of willows. In it were two paddles and a parcel of grease. The canoe had been left here for Mr. Hardisty, who was expected back from an eastern visit.

It was late on a Saturday evening when we camped upon the shore, and my companions were almost paralyzed by the appearance of the river. They had all day Sunday to become familiar with the sight of this mad current and its tremendous volume of water.

Monday morning I was up with the day, and calling my two men we boiled the kettle, chopped some chunks from our mass of pemmican, and sat down to breakfast. Presently Mr. Connor crawled out of his cart, and sitting on its edge, said, "Good morning."

I invited him to a cup of tea and a piece of pemmican, but to my astonishment he very solemnly said, "Before I do anything today I want to come to an agreement with you men as to how long you are prepared to stay here and search for the body of anyone of us who may be drowned here today."

Oliver dropped his pemmican; his eyes widened and his face blanched. I saw that I must do something or else I would not be able to take Oliver near the river that day. So, I laughed out a regular "Ha, ha!" at the old man's strange demand.

"It is no laughing matter," said he.

"Yes," I answered, "it is — a very laughable matter, that a man of your age and experience should make such a proposition. In the first place we do not expect anyone to be drowned here today. More, if any of us should drown in that current, what would be the use of searching for the body? If I am the one to be drowned, don't you lose a minute looking for my body, but go on taking the stuff across and get it to its destination.

"But take my word for it, we will get across all right. Come along and have a cup of tea."

This he did without saying any more about drowning, and he worked like a trooper all the rest of the day, helping in any way he could. Some years later, Mr. Connor was drowned.

Breakfast over, we immediately began operations. The first thing was to carry the canoe to the water's edge. Then we bit off a mouthful of grease, chewed it until it became like gum, and used it to cover all the seams of the canoe.

We launched the canoe and for the first trip across put in two men and about three hundred pounds. As the current would carry us down a great distance while crossing, we had to track or trail our canoe up the river a long way. This we did by one pulling on a line and the other wading along the shore and keeping the canoe out from the rocks. When we did let go, the two in the canoe had to paddle as hard as they could, for the rough hide and flat shape of the clumsy thing made it very heavy in the water.

Having reached the other side, we unloaded and carried up our goods out of the reach of a possible rise of water. Again we had to pull our canoe a long way up the river on that side to reach anywhere near our starting point. After the first trip we found that we could average about four hundred pounds with the two men. So, keeping hard at it the long summer's day, drying our boat while we lunched or dined or supped, and ever and anon repitching it with the grease, we had most of our stuff across by sundown and were once more in camp — and no one drowned!

The next morning we pulled our carts as far up the river as there was beach to move on, and then, crossing over several times, we got the remainder of our freight, harness, and camping outfit across.

In the meantime we were making a raft of the carts. We took the wheels off and fastened them to the boxes and tied the whole together. My plan was to fasten one end of a long rope to the raft and carefully coil up the rest in the canoe. Then a third man in the canoe would pay it out while two of us paddled for the other side as fast as possible. Once there, we would jump out and with the rope gently warp our raft to the shore. But that current was strong and treacherous, and when after a fearful struggle we did succeed in reaching the opposite bank, to my dismay the rope broke at the first strain. Away went our raft of carts.

There was just one spot, about a mile down, where we could land those carts. If we missed that, the current would sweep them to the other side of the river and on into a series of rapids below. To jump into the canoe, to chase that raft, to hitch to it, and then to paddle for the shore as we went at a furious rate on that swirling, seething, boiling torrent was our instant action.

How we worked! How I watched that one spot where it was possible for us to land! How I calculated the time when I would pay out the line, and once more try to warp our raft in! How as by a miracle we did make the one spot, and held our raft, and, securing it, sat down on the shore rested, and were thankful!

Our difficulties were not yet over. We had heavy work before us to take those carts out of the spot where we landed. We would have to climb a steep, almost perpendicular bank covered with brush, then make a road of some two or three miles in order to reach the spot where our goods were. The first thing to be done was to take the carts out of the water and put them together. Then, by wading and tracking and pulling and pushing, we had to take the heavy skin canoe upstream and cross once again, as our stock were still on the south side.

Now came the tug of war, for those cattle were afraid of the wide stream and the strong current. We drove them up and started them in at the spot where the flow of water struck for the other side. All in vain, they kept coming back on us. We shouted and waded in after them. Many times we gave them a fresh send-off.

Finally we towed one over after the canoe, and rushed the balance in after this one, but they went back on us again. We took another, and still the rest would not follow. At last, after hours of the hardest kind of work, we got them to strike out and swim across, some of them going a long distance downstream.

At a late hour on Tuesday evening we were camped—goods and carts and stock and men—on the north side of the south branch, and as yet no one drowned! To say we were thankful is to say but little. Even the seemingly emotionless Scot of our party unbent that evening and became quite funny. But we were also very tired. The soles of my feet were badly cut with the sharp stones and the fine sand had got into the wounds, causing me intense pain.

The next morning I depended on Oliver and Jim to hunt up the stock, for my feet were badly swollen and only with great difficulty could I put them to the ground. After being hours away, they returned and reported the most of our horses lost. There was nothing else for me to do but to soak my swollen feet and moccasins in the river and start out to look for them.

By taking a big circle from the river, I finally found their track. Running or walking or crawling depending on the nature of the soil and the grass, I followed them up. Sometimes I was obliged to go on my hands and knees in order to detect the faint tracks left by those unshod horses. After hours of such tracking and of closest scanning of the track, I came to the summit of a hill and was exceedingly fortunate in catching a glimpse of my horses disappearing over the brow of a hill in the distance.

Seeing them saved me hours and enabled me to catch up on them fast, for I did not stop running until I reached the spot where they had disappeared from view. As they were not in sight, I began tracking again and very soon came to the truants in a swamp. I caught one, and jumping on bare-back, made those horses fairly fly back to the river. I was gladly welcomed by my companions, who had become anxious at my long absence. Working on into the night, we succeeded in climbing the hill, and camped about three miles from the river.

The next day we reached Carlton and the North Saskatchewan. Here we had a wider river to cross, but were fortunate in securing the loan of a boat. It was old and very leaky, yet it enabled us to cross a cart and its load at each trip. Our cattle did not give us so much trouble as at the south branch. We were not quite two days in crossing. Here we had a long, high hill to double up with our loads, but finally we were on the top of it.

We were on the home side of the two big Saskatchewans, and I was a glad man because of it. The hundreds of miles yet to travel, the many smaller rivers and streams yet to cross, seemed as nothing to what we had passed. The backbone of the trip was now broken.

The same afternoon that we left the north side of the river, I came across an Indian who took a strong fancy to the horse I was riding, the one I had broken in the lake. Though a fine animal, it had caused me a deal of trouble and had no doubt taken the lead in going so far a few days before. As the Indian had a stout grey horse which he said was good in the harness, we agreed to "swap even." So, dismounting, we changed our saddles from one horse to the other and each went his own way satisfied. My grey pony proved himself first-class in the cart.

Across wide valleys, over great ranges of hills, we rolled westward, reached and passed the rendezvous of the threatening Jackfish Lake Indians. I was glad to note that there were no fresh tracks in the vicinity. They were either out on the plains after buffalo or in the north hunting moose. As we had a very small party, I had felt anxious about these people.

The next day, however, our number was strengthened by unexpectedly meeting Father and Peter. Going to Fort Pitt on missionary work, Father had met Ka-kake, who had told him that I could not be very many days behind; so, he had come on. As we were now getting farther into the country frequented by war parties from the south, it was a comfort and joy to have our little party so handsomely reinforced.

Father was pleased with my purchases of cattle and complimented me on the condition of the stock. He thought we could afford to push them, as they would have plenty of time to fatten for winter after we reached the mission. From daylight until dark, stopping only to feed, we kept at it and made good time.

The old landmarks of the bridle-path across the continent — Red Deer Hill, Frenchman's Butte, Fort Pitt, Two Hills, Moose Creek, the Dog Rump, Egg Lake — each in turn was left behind.

We had reached the limit of wheel tracks on the north side of the Saskatchewan. We were about fifty miles or more from Victoria, and our party would have to make the trail the rest of the way through new country. In our camp on the home side of Egg Lake, Father said to me, "John, you may gallop on to the mission in the morning and see your mother and sisters. And if you can find them, bring us some fresh horses."

Early the next morning found me astride of my little sorrel — the one the Indians had named "The Scarred Thigh" because he had once been tossed by a mad buffalo — and away we went on the steady jump. Before noon we were at the mission, joyfully welcomed by Mother and friends. Part of that afternoon I spent at home with Mother, and during part of it hunted up our horses and corralled them for the night.

The new house was finished and Mother was comfortably settled once more in a substantial home. It was without any furniture or stoves, but Larsen was hard at work at the former, and time and money would eventually bring the latter. The stockade around the mission house was finished; another field had been fenced, broken, and planted; the prospect of a garden crop was good, and our chance of barley for soup next winter was largely possible. I saw, too, a number of garden patches that the Indians had fenced in, hoed, and planted with the small share of seeds the mission could give them. This was their very first effort to till the land.

Mr. Woolsey had returned to Ontario. I missed his genial, kindly presence. For nearly a decade, from 1855 to 1864, this devoted servant of God had journeyed incessantly up and down through the length and breadth of the Upper Saskatchewan and among the foot-hills of the Rockies. He had mastered the syllabic system so that he could read and write in it, and also teach to others the use of this wonderful invention which God gave to James Evans. I had been Mr. Woolsey's interpreter, guide, and general "roust-about," his confidante and friend for two years. Now that he was gone, I felt a twinge of melancholy.

The next day I started back with some fresh horses and met our party coming along famously. For picking a road Peter was a genius. All hands worked willingly in chopping out the road, brushing swamps, and bridging creeks. Late in the evening of the following day we rolled down the hill into the beautiful valley of the Saskatchewan at Victoria, ours the first carts to ascend the north side of that great river so far west as this point.

Fifty-six travelling days from Fort Garry — stock all right, carts sound, goods dry, and twenty-five pounds of flour still left in the bag we began on when we left the Red River settlements — such was our record. Father was pleased. Because he was pleased, I was happy. Mother, the children, and Larsen luxuriated in hot rolls for supper. She saw a Christmas pudding and no end of cake for the many sick folks whom she so much delighted to minister to. My sisters laughed and our little baby brother gleefully shouted, "Cake! Plenty cake!" The cows assured us of milk and butter, and if other resources failed, of beef also.

Of those who came with me from Red River, the Scotchman traded his cart and harness to Father and, packing his horse, went on to Edmonton. He took the trail through the Yellowhead Pass for British Columbia, never to be heard of by us again. Mr. Connor and his son concluded to winter beside us, and went to work putting up a shanty to live in.

One mishap had come upon us during my absence. A forest and prairie fire which came in from the south, "like a wolf on the fold," had burnt our saw-pit and saws, together with considerable lumber. This was quite a set-back, as the manufacture of lumber by hand is slow work. Having more stock necessitated our making more hay and providing more stable room. Then we went to work at replacing the timber and lumber which had been burnt.

Our purpose now was to build, as soon as possible, a church.

SIXTEEN

Indian Friends

With the advance of autumn our Indian friends began to gather to the mission. Maskepetoon's Wood Crees arrived. They were followed by many of the Plains Crees. For days the river banks and crossing in front of the mission house were alive. Horses there were in many hundreds, of all colours and grades, and dogs, it seemed, by the thousands. Incessant shoutings and neighings and howlings broke the quiet of our valley. The smoke of myriad lodges hung over the scene.

During the summer a number of skirmishes had taken place between the Crees and the Blackfeet. Scalps had been taken home and rejoiced over in both camps. Warriors had gone straight from the field of blood to the "Big Sand Hills," as the Blackfoot would say, or to the "Happier Spirit Land." Many a young fellow who had no horse last spring now rejoices in the ownership of a little band. Successful stealing gives him a place among men.

Both Father and Mother have taken a strong liking to Maskepetoon and have given the old gentleman a room in the new house. In this room, of which he is very proud, he leaves his paper and books and clothes, and into it he often goes to read his Bible. His manly, courteous and kindly behaviour makes it pleasant to have him in the house. In every good work he is the missionary's right hand.

At this time the missionary needs all the help he can secure. This strange, promiscuous, turbulent crowd need careful handling. Men who quarreled about a horse or a woman brought the case to the missionary to settle. Women whose husbands had, as they say, "thrown them away," came to him to reinstate them in their husband's favour and lodge. Widows who had been robbed by their late husband's relatives poured their complaints into his ear, and looked to him to adjust their claims. Monogamy *versus* polygamy was a burning question, and very often the preacher was sorely puzzled to know what to do in the matter. All the sick in camp expected the praying man to help them.

What with meetings all through the week and almost all day Sunday, Father and Peter were constantly employed.

Then came the solemn gathering of the big council, when the long-stemmed pipe was passed around and every rite and ceremony religiously observed. These council gatherings were fine opportunities for the missionary who, if in the vicinity and if he had the confidence of the people, was always invited to be present. At these would assemble both friends and foes. Conjurers and medicine men were there, who felt their craft was in danger. Warriors and horse-thieves, too, who loved their life of wild lawlessness, and readily foresaw that if this new faith should have sway their present mode of life would cease.

Others were there who intensely hated the white man. His cupidity, sensuality, and generally aggressive conduct had at some time in their history insulted and wronged their whole being, and now they fairly loathed the sight of the white portion of the race. On the other hand were the few who had embraced the new faith and who were in hearty sympathy with the mission.

War, peace, trade, the present, the future, their old faiths, the new one brought in by these missionaries, all these matters would be discussed at the councils. The tactful exponent of Gospel teaching would watch his chance, and from the speeches and arguments of his audience turn the trend of thought to Christianity and civilization.

It was fortunate that our mission had a strong friend and ally such as Maskepetoon. With consummate tact he would preside over these council gatherings, and in every one of them score a point or more in favour of the missionary and the cause he represented.

It is related of Maskepetoon that after he had become renowned as a victorious warrior — when the Blackfeet tribes had given him the name of Mon-e-guh-ba-now or the Young Chief — his aged father said to him, "My son, you are making a great mistake. The glory you are now seeking will be short-lived. Delighting in war and taking pleasure in the spilling of man's blood is all wrong. If you want to be a great man, if you want to be remembered long, turn about and work for peace. This is the only thing that will give you true fame."

Six different times did this heathen philosopher thus address his beloved son. But Maskepetoon's young manhood was lived at a time when the rich premiums of love, respect, gratitude were lavishly bestowed upon the perfect horseman, successful hunter, and the brave and victorious warrior. This proud and haughty youthful chieftain would fold his arms around his head and, bowing himself, would sit in silent reverence and meekly listen. But his warlike spirit would rebel against this sage advice.

Yet his father's words troubled him. At last he filled a pipe and went over to the lodge of an aged man, said to be wise beyond the wisdom of other men. Lighting the pipe, he handed it to the old man. He asked for counsel as to what was best in life and what was evil and should be shunned. The humble-minded old Indian said, "Your father is more capable of advising you than I am."

Maskepetoon persisted. Then the aged philosopher cut eight small sticks of different lengths and stood them in the ground, four in a row.

"These sticks," said this unschooled professor of ethics, "represent two lines of life. I will give them names. These four are falsehood, dishonesty, hatred of fellow men, war. Those are truth, honesty, love of fellow men, peace. I will speak of each one.

I want you to open your ears and treasure in your heart what I have to say."

When the old man had finished talking to his intent young listener, he gathered the line of sticks ending in war, and said, "Shall we keep these, or shall I burn them?"

"Burn them," Maskepetoon replied.

"Shall I bind these others ending in peace together and give them to you in remembrance of what I have told you?"

"Bind them well and give them to me." And thus Maskepetoon forsook war and became the champion of peace. In this way he became the forerunner of the Gospel of Peace, which in a few years was to be preached for the first time in this new land.

In the meantime Maskepetoon's reformation was put to severe tests by the murder of his friends and fellow tribesmen, and by the frequent stealing of his horses. But he stood firm. Then came the killing of his father by the Blackfeet. Friends and foes, knowing him as they did, watched and wondered. He was immovable, and remained loyal to his new position as the apostle of peace in this lawless country.

Soon after Maskepetoon placed himself upon record before all men as "Peace Chief." It happened while he and his people were encamped near Peace Hills, close to where the town of Wetaskewin now stands. A large party of Blackfeet and their allies came in on their way to trade at Fort Edmonton. Under such circumstances the Blackfeet were only too glad to ask for a temporary peace, and this being arranged they came into the Cree camp, seemingly forgetful that they had with them the very man who had killed Maskepetoon's father. Somehow this came out and caused consternation in the minds of both parties. Said they, "If the young chief hears this, then there will be terrible war."

Maskepetoon did find out that the man who had killed his parent was in his camp. When he heard it, he sent for his best horse, had him saddled and accoutred as for war, and fastened him at his tent door. Intense anxiety prevailed, and all were nerved up for the struggle which they thought inevitable. Maskepetoon sent for his father's murderer. The man, an elderly warrior, came as to his death. Maskepetoon waved him to a seat near himself in the tent. Passing him his own adorned chief's clothes, made of leather, decorated with beads and quills and fringed with human hair, he said to him, "Put those on."

"Now," thought the frightened yet stolid murderer, "he is only dressing me out for my death." Brave men on both sides held their breath as they looked on, calmly making ready for the desperate struggle they believed was coming.

Again Maskepetoon spoke. "You deprived me of my father, and there was a time when I would have gloried in taking your life and in drinking your blood. That is past. What makes you pale? You need not fear; I will not kill you. You must now be to me as a father. Wear my clothes, ride my horse. And tell your people when you go back to your camp this is the way Mon-e-guh-ba-now takes revenge."

Then the old Blackfoot found speech and said, "You have killed me, my son. You are a great man. Never in the history of my people has such as this you have done been known. My people and all men will hear of this and say, 'The young chief is brave and strong and good. He stands alone.'"

When the English Wesleyan Conference sent the Rev. R. T. Rundle to labour amongst the Indians of the Hudson's Bay Territory, Maskepetoon met him at Rocky Mountain House. Then the missionary visited his camp at Burnt Lake. Later on Maskepetoon learned the syllabic system, taught him by Mr. Harriott, an officer of the Hudson's Bay Company who was stationed for some time at the Mountain Fort. Then he became a student of the New Testament, translated by Steinhauer and Sinclair into a dialect of his mother tongue. From that day Maskepetoon took sides with the Gospel and became the true friend of the missionary.

Muh-ka-chees, or "the Fox," was another particular friend of ours, but one who clung to his old faith.

He was quite a wag in his way. He created a hearty laugh around our campfire by describing an imaginary scene, in which he was to have settled down beside the mission and gone into farming and stock-raising, while the crowd around him would go on in the old way, hunting and trapping. He would become wealthy, adopt the white man's mode of life, dress, etc. Then one day it would be reported that the York boats with their crews were coming up the river from their long and slavish trip to the Coast, the men in harness and working like beasts of burden — as they were. He would drop his work for a bit and dress up in a neat-cut coat and white shirt. With hat cocked on one side just a little, and tobacco rolled like a stick in his mouth, with cane in hand, he would walk down to the river bank. As the boats came up he would carelessly look over at his old companions, still in their primitive costume and slaving for others while he was independent. Then holding the rolled tobacco between two fingers and turning on his heel, he would say, "Only a lot of savages, anyway," and go back to his comfortable home.

The point in the joke was that, of the crowd around the campfire, the Fox was the least likely to change in a hurry.

He was said to be able to transform himself in case of necessity into a fox. The "spirit of his dream" — the power to whom he was under vow — had given him assurance that in his hour of extremity this spirit would come to his help and enable him to change his visible appearance — the man Fox would become the animal fox in shape.

This, it was told me, had actually taken place, and an eyewitness thus described the circumstances:

"The Fox and four others of us started out in the late autumn to steal horses or take scalps from the Blackfeet. The Fox was our leader and conjurer. Now and then he was to look into the unknown and determine our course and movements. We left our camps between the Battle River and the North Saskatchewan and travelled south for several days. We crossed the Red Deer below the big canyon and came to the track of a large camp of Blackfeet travelling southerly.

"Now we began to move with extreme caution, and when south of Service Berry Creek, I went on alone to scout. As the tracks were fresh, my companions remained hidden while I was away. After a long, stealthy run I came in sight of the camp of the enemy. Taking stock of it and its locality, I went back to my companions. I hoped to inspire them with great enthusiasm because of what I had seen. Though I sang the war song as I approached them, they did not stir. I saw a gloom was upon the party.

"Then the Fox spoke up and said, 'I am sorry, but it is no use; we must return from here. The Spirit has informed me that it would be utter ruin for us to advance. We must retrace our steps.' I was loath to do this. I wanted horses. I scolded Fox for deceiving us; but he was determined, as he said, to follow the guidance of the one he dreamt of. Already my comrades had started on the back trail. Sullenly and quietly we moved northward.

"Presently the Fox began to limp, and then sat down saying, 'There is something in my knee. See if you can find a thorn or a splinter.' We could not find any such thing and yet his knee was swollen and inflamed. Soon he could not put his foot to the ground. He said to us repeatedly, 'Leave me, let me die alone.' But we would not listen to that. I made him a crutch, and we moved on slowly, very slowly. We helped him from time to time, but his leg grew worse, and was terribly swollen.

"And now winter came upon us and snow and cold increased. When we reached the Red Deer it was frozen out on both sides and the channel was full of float ice. I said, 'I will cross first and have a fire ready for you.' So I stripped, forded the river, and made a camp on the north side in a clump of spruce. When this was ready, I shouted to my companions to come across. They took a long pole, and put the Fox in the centre, and all holding on to the pole waded abreast through the current and float ice.

"The snow was now deep and we were out of provisions. The next morning my brother and myself went to hunt for game. We had not gone far when we saw tracks in the snow which turned out to be those of buffalo. I succeeded in killing two. Our party packed all of the meat into our camp, and we busied ourselves in cutting up and drying this meat for our journey.

"In the meantime the Fox's leg was growing worse, and he implored us to abandon him, but we could not do this. I fixed a strap of buffalo-hide to go across his shoulder, and fastening this to two crutches, we made another start. Climbing the steep banks of the Red Deer, and with many stops, we continued our way homeward. Our course was along the Buffalo Lake.

"One day we heard shooting in the distance, and scouting for the cause we found that a Sarcee camp was right in our way. This was very disappointing, as it compelled us to make a big detour to avoid this camp and its many hunters. Very slowly and stealthily we travelled among our enemies. There was no chance to steal horses because the snow was too deep and our party was too weak. They would be able to track us at once and our scalps would certainly be theirs. Several times we were nearly discovered, but the weather, being cold and stormy and at times misty, favoured us.

"When we had got about opposite the camp, my brother filled a pipe and, handing it to the Fox, said to him, 'Here, smoke that and call upon your source of help; for you need this now as we are likely to be tracked or seen at any time.' So the Fox smoked the pipe and said, 'Well, leave me here alone and hurry on to yonder woods. Do not look back, but wait for me when you reach the woods.'

"We left him and ran across the plain. I was ahead and did not look back. But as we ran all of a sudden I heard my brother cry out, 'Alas! I have injured the Fox,' and without looking back, I said, 'What is it?' And my brother told me that he had looked back and seen the Fox coming on the dead run after us, but while he looked he saw him fall as if struck down. Then he knew he had broken the charm or influence by his disobedience.

"When we reached the woods we waited. After a long time the Fox crawled up and at once charged us with looking back. 'I was coming on nicely when you looked back and spoiled me by your foolish curiosity.' My brother confessed at once that it was he who had done this. But, he said, he was prompted to do so because he had been left alone and our enemies might come upon him at any time.

"After this the Fox got worse and his foot and all of his leg was fearfully swollen. I could not find any gathering of matter. After days of slow progress the weather became milder and in some spots on the hills the snow went off. One day we came out upon the valley which is called, 'Where the buffalo hunters meet in running.' We sat down on the hill above the valley.

"Here, I thought, I will try the Fox and see if there is anything in his boasted association with the spirits. So, I filled a pipe, lighted it, and said to him, 'Here, smoke this, and listen to me. You brought us out on this trip. You promised us horses. You led us to depend on your spiritual power. You have deceived us in every way, and for many days you have been a burden to us. Many times our lives have been in danger because of you. Why continue this any longer? Why not invoke the help you profess to be able to call to your aid? Do this now.'

"Then the Fox said, 'Your words are true. You should have left me to die long ago, but you would not. I have been a burden and a danger to you. I will do as you say; possibly I may be heard.' Baring his back, he said, 'Here, paint a fox on my back with this yellow earth. Let my head represent his head, let his forelegs go down onto my arms, and his hind legs onto my thighs. Make my head and back yellow, then take some powder and wet it, and darken the lower parts of his limbs and tail, and my nose and mouth, and take a little white earth and tip the tail.' I and my companions did as he told us.

"Then he said, 'Cross the valley, climb the hill. Just over its brow wait for me. But mind, as you cross the valley and climb the hill, do not look back — remember that.' Then he held the pipe on high and began to chant his invocation song. Thus we left him. Nor did we look back as we ran across the valley in which the buffalo were standing on both sides of us like a black wall. Climbing the hill, we went over its brow, and made a circle so as to command our track, and there we waited. We were intensely anxious.

"By and by we saw a stir among the buffalo in the valley. Then we discerned a small object coming on our track. It looked in the distance like a kit fox, and when nearer it appeared like an ordinary red fox. On it came at the gallop and, keeping our track, climbed the hill and was soon on its brow. Presently it was opposite to us.

"We were now in full view. Then it saw us. The Fox himself rose up, saying, 'Ah, you caught me in my other self.' We did not say anything, we were so astonished. The Fox walked over to us as if there were nothing the matter with him. His leg, which had been big and swollen, was now down to its usual size. He pulled his legging down and said to me, 'Here, lance this, and I will be all right.' Sure enough, there was a bag of matter on his knee, but the swelling was gone. So I took an arrow, sharpened the point, bound it around with string a little distance from the point, and with it lanced his knee. The matter poured forth. Then I made a ring of twisted grass, bound this over the wound, and we continued the journey.

"The Fox delayed us no more, and in a few days was entirely recovered."

Another of our friends was called "The-Camp-is-Moving." He would shake his powder-horn and it would never empty. Like the widow's cruse of oil, it would replenish. It was said he had but to sing and shake his horn, and powder came at his bidding. Once he came to me at Pigeon Lake and begged for some shot. "You know," said he, "I am all right as to powder," giving his powder-horn a significant shake. I ventured to say that it might be easier to make shot than powder and that if I could make powder I would try making shot also. "Ah, my grandchild," said the old man, "we must not be presuming. I am thankful that it is given to me to make powder." After that, what could I do but give him some shot.

These men and others widely differing from us in creed were friendly and kind in their attitude to the people of our mission.

SEVENTEEN

Maskepetoon: Peacemaker

The Indians, both Wood and Plains, pagan and Christian, were now flocking into Victoria in such numbers that the Hudson's Bay Company saw the necessity of establishing a trading post there. I was offered the charge of this, but Father did not seem to relish the idea; so it dropped and a Mr. Flett was sent to put up buildings and open trade with the Indians. Mr. Flett was a native of the Red River settlement and thoroughly understood the Indians and their language. He was a warm friend of our mission, later on himself becoming an honoured missionary of the Presbyterian Church to the Indians in another part of the country.

As autumn merged into winter, the larger number of the Indians recrossed the Saskatchewan and struck for the buffalo. In the meantime some of us were busy getting out more timber and lumber.

As the cold weather set in, it became necessary to organize for the "fresh meat hunt." This time our course was more westerly. On the third day we had our first run near the "cross woods," on the plain which stretches from within a few miles of Victoria to the Battle River. Our chief hunters were "Muddy Bull" and Peter. The rest of us were kept busy butchering and hauling into camp, moving, guarding stock, providing wood, etc. From before daylight until late at night we were all on the jump, Sunday being our only rest, and then we took turns in guarding our stock.

On the third evening, after we got fairly among the buffalo, our carts were loaded and we felt that we had been successful indeed. No lives lost, no limbs broken, no horses stolen. Our hunters had ridden without hurt over thousands of badger holes, across many miles of rough country, and amongst hundreds of wild, strong buffalo. Our cart drivers had gone in every direction, to and fro across country, butchering the slain, and hauling in the meat to camp. Hundreds of great grey wolves, and—to judge by the yelping—thousands of coyotes, had howled and snarled and fought all about us both day and night.

In those days we seldom bothered with the hides. Now and then we took some specially good ones and used them on the way home to cover the meat, and later on had them dressed. But generally, with the exception of what we used to mend carts or harness, we left the hides on the plain. Our need was meat, and for this we required the utmost capacity of our transport.

On these trips we tried to be away as briefly as possible; for the mission, during our absence, was almost without any protection. So our carts were soon creaking and squealing with their heavy loads on the home stretch.

Winter was steadily creeping on. The ground was frozen, the ice on the lakes becoming thick and strong, and the nights were cold. If you were on guard, you felt the need for action to keep warm. If you were asleep under the carts, you very reluctantly turned out at four o'clock in the morning to gather up bedding, etc., hitch up your share of the brigade, and trudge through the cold until near daylight, when you stopped for breakfast. The chicken-hearted and weak-willed had no place in this new land.

In a little more than two weeks from our start on the hunt, we were again letting our loads down the steep southern bank of the Saskatchewan. Back home once more we found plenty to do in making ready for winter. There were cattle to provide for and look after, horses to keep track of, dogs to feed, wood to cut, haul, and again split up at the door, timber to take out, and lumber to saw, dry, plane, groove and tongue.

In the meantime Peter married a Whitefish Lake woman and brought her to the mission. She was a fine-looking Christian woman, and we all congratulated our friend on his good fortune. Mr. Connor, who came up with me from the Red River in the summer, and whom I left some time since building a shack for the winter, took the work of harvesting and threshing our small field of barley on shares.

He also engaged to teach school for the winter months. Our shanty is to be the schoolroom, and Mr. Steinhauer's children from Whitefish Lake, our family, and a few orphan Indian children are to be the scholars. This will be the first institution of the kind in this part of the North-West. Father accepted the little daughter of "Chief Child," who in dying besought him to take his much loved child and train her in a Christian home. Thus our home will send nine scholars to the new school. For the winter months Mother's responsibility will increase greatly, while we who have to provide food will have to keep on the move.

Our garden this year had given us a nice quantity of potatoes and we have some barley, but meat will be our chief food. As we have no mill, the only way we can prepare barley is to soak it, and when it is partly dry to pound it in a wooden mortar to loosen the chaff and husks, and then to winnow this. We boil the barley in soup, or else parch it and grind it in our small coffee-mill, and make cake of the meal. All of this is slow and tedious work. So long as we can get buffalo within three hundred miles we would prefer buffalo-steaks to barley meal.

About the first of December, snow came. Father had decided to begin a mission on Pigeon Lake between Edmonton and the mountains. He told me that he wanted me to look up the place and if it was possible to prepare some timber for a house, as he proposed to do something in the coming spring in the way of a permanent occupancy. The Mountain and Wood Stoneys and some Wood Crees who frequented that country were without a missionary.

Accordingly, early in December I took Oliver with me and started with two trains of dogs, carrying loads of dried provisions. In two days we reached Edmonton. I hired as guide the one half-breed around the Fort who had ever been at Pigeon Lake.

During the evening I went to see how my guide was progressing in making ready for a start in the morning. I found him both sick and lame. I thought this strange and set to work to find the secret cause of such a change. His spiritual adviser had put his foot on our enterprise — as he thought.

"Will we go back?" enquired Oliver.

"No, sir," I said, "we will find Pigeon Lake notwithstanding all the priests in Canada."

With the creaking of the heavy gates on their hinges, we drove out of the Fort in the morning. The plan I had formed in the night was to follow a trail which led from Edmonton to the Mountain House until we came to Battle River, then to follow this up to Pigeon Creek, which ran out of Pigeon Lake. We would follow the creek to the lake and coast along the shore until I found the spot where it was proposed to establish a mission. This was a long distance around.

Away we went, all day on the south-bound trail, and camped for the night in a clump of spruce. Then, as the track could be plainly seen, we were off before daylight and before noon came upon a new-made road crossing ours at right angles. Here I stopped and pondered. If this road came from Pigeon Lake, it would save us four or five days' journey in going and coming.

"Here goes," I said to Oliver, "we will take this trail and follow it until tomorrow night or to its end. At the worst we can come back and take up our original plan." So we turned up the new road and carried on faster than ever. Now we were travelling almost due west through forest. When it came time to stop for the night, I selected a suitable place, pulled my dogs out of their collars, and left Oliver to make camp. After running some distance, I climbed a tree and took a survey of the country. It was all forest and no sign of a lake to be seen.

Paul Kane

Half Breed Encampment

Next morning we were away early and by noon had climbed a range of hills covered with dense timber. On reaching the summit we noticed a big depression not far ahead. It was Pigeon Lake. In about an hour we were on the ice and driving across the bay to our destination. The Indians had cached some fish, which we used for our dogs. We spent the rest of the day in fixing up a camp.

In three days we had nearly enough timber for two modest houses. We had not far to haul it, our dogs were quick, and we were both of us fairly good axemen. We cached our provisions, took some fish instead, and started about two o'clock one moonlit morning on our return trip. More snow had fallen and the roads were heavier; nevertheless, we made Edmonton the same evening before the gates closed. Every Protestant in the Fort was glad we had found Pigeon Lake. We spent most of the next day with friends at the Fort and in the evening, just before the gates closed, drove out some five miles and camped for the night. Starting early next morning we made a trail through several inches of new snow, and between seven and eight we had reached the mission house.

Father was delighted with our report of the trip. We had found the lake, got out the timber, cached the provisions, and in a sense started the new mission.

As our stock of meat was now growing small, Father thought I had better go out to the plains and see how things were among the Indians, and if possible bring in a supply of meat. So, very soon after coming from Pigeon Lake, I arranged a party for the purpose. Old Joseph and a young Indian named Tommy went with me. James Connor came with us on his own account. We had four trains of dogs. The third day out we came to Maskepetoon's camp and found the Indians full of stories of another of the old Chief's plucky deeds.

During the late fall and early winter, the Blackfeet had become exceedingly troublesome; they were continually harassing the Wood Cree camp. At last Maskepetoon determined to go with a party to the Blackfeet camp to arrange, if possible, a temporary peace which might last the winter and thus give the Crees an opportunity to make robes and provisions for trade and home use.

As winter advanced, the buffalo had come north rapidly, and the Blackfeet tribes had of necessity to follow them. Fearful destitution had been the result to some of the large camps. They had eaten their dogs and begun upon their horses before they reached the south fringe of the large herds that were moving north into the rich and well-sheltered areas of the Saskatchewan country. It was well known in Maskepetoon's camp that the Blackfeet were in strength not more than one hundred miles south, and that the Bloods and Piegans were within easy distance beyond them.

Maskepetoon had great faith in his record with these people. At the head of a small party he set out to patch up a peace, even if it should be but short-lived. His little band was charged by a strong body of Blackfeet who were coming north on the warpath. Such was their number and the vigour and dash of their charge that Maskepetoon's company fled, all but himself and his grandson, a boy some fifteen or sixteen years of age.

The veteran chief and the noble boy stood like statues. Maskepetoon calmly put his hand in his bosom and took out his Cree Testament, and then coolly fixing on his glasses, opened and began to read. The grandson, in relating to us the incident afterwards, said, "There was no tremor in his voice. It was as if grandfather was reading to us in the quiet of his own tent."

The Blackfeet came on apace but, hoping to take their victims alive, refrained from firing a gun or speeding an arrow. Then they saw the majestic old man, indifferent to them, engaged in looking into something he held in his hand. They had faced flintlock guns, and flint and steel-shod arrows, but they had never beheld a New Testament. They paused in their wild rush and stared in utter astonishment.

Presently the elders amongst them said to one another in whispers, "It is Mon-e-guh-ba-now," and then they began to shout his name. This grand old man quietly looked up and in response to their shout, replied, "Yes, I am Mon-e-guh-ba-now."

Then they rushed upon him with joy, and their leader, embracing him, said, "Our hearts are glad to make peace with you, Mon-e-guh-ba-now. You are a brave man. I am proud and glad to be the leader of a party that meets you thus. What is that you hold in your hand?" Maskepetoon told him that it was the word of the Great Spirit, and the Blackfoot warrior said, "That explains your conduct. It is His will that we should meet as brothers today."

And there on the snow-covered plain, these men, who by heredity and life-long habit were deadly enemies, smoked and talked and planned for peace. It was arranged that each party should return to their own people, and that if the Blackfeet desired peace they should send an embassy to the Cree camp. Maskepetoon gave his word as a guarantee for the safety of those who might be sent on this errand.

This had occurred a few days before our arrival in camp, and the Blackfeet were expected at any moment. Hardly were we settled in Muddy Bull's hospitable lodge, when a scout reached camp and announced that a party of Blackfeet were in sight. This threw the camp into a state of great excitement. Speculation was rife as to whether Maskepetoon would be able to make good his promise of safety. There were hundreds in that camp who lusted and thirsted for the blood of these men; many a boy or girl who had lost a father or mother or both; many a woman who had lost lover or husband; many parents who had lost their children at the hands of the people represented by these men who were now approaching camp. Many of these felt down in their hearts that this would be a fine opportunity to slake some of their thirst for revenge.

Maskepetoon at once sent his son out to meet the embassy and attend them into camp. In the meantime he stationed his trusted men all through the camp to be ready to forestall any outbreak of frenzied hate.

I ran out to see the incoming of the Blackfeet. Young Maskepetoon had arranged an escort. These men were on horseback and ranged on either side of the Blackfeet who were on foot. The latter were seven in number, big, fine-looking fellows; but one could see that they were under a heavy strain and that it needed all their will-power to nerve them up to the occasion. With regular and solemn step, in single file they came. As they walked they sang what I supposed was intended for a peace song. Young Maskepetoon took them straight to his father's lodge, and at once it was arranged to hold a reception meeting and a "peace dance."

At supper I enquired of old Joseph what he thought of my attending this dance. He said he was not going himself, but he thought Maskepetoon would like to have me there, and that I had better go and see for myself, so as to learn all I could about the Indians, for only in this way would I get to understand them. So, when the drums beat to announce the dance, I went and was given a seat between Maskepetoon and the Blackfeet. Two large lodges had been put together to make room, but the main body of the company looked on from the outside.

After a few short speeches the dancing began. Four men drummed and sang, and an Indian sprang into the ring between the fire and the guests, leaped, jumped, and whooped with great spirit, and presently gave his blanket to one of the Blackfeet. Then another did likewise, except that he varied the gift. This time it was his beaded shot-pouch and powder-horn, and strings also. Each one, it would seem, had his own peculiar dance. Then another would leap into the ring with several articles, and as he danced to the strong singing and vigorous drumming of the orchestra, he would give to a Blackfoot his contributions to this peace meeting.

Then the drummers ceased for a little and the conductor shouted out, "The Sloping Bank is strong for peace. He had but one blanket and he has given that." "The Red Sky Bird means what he says. He had but one gun and he has given that." And again the leader tapped his drum and the orchestra burst forth and another and yet another dancer took the floor. Then a couple of young fellows, in fantastic costume, gave us the "buffalo dance," and did some tall jumping that would have pleased one of those "highly cultured audiences" of our eastern cities.

Presently my friend, Mr. Starving Bull, took the floor. He was no small man, this Mr. Starving Bull. He had several new blankets on his shoulders, and a brand-new flint-lock gun in his hand. As he danced and whooped and kept time to the furious drumming, he gave his gun to one of the Blackfeet as he whirled past him, and again gave one of the new blankets to another. And so on, until he had spent all his gifts and strength and sat down naked and tired. Then the chief singer shouted out his name, and said, "The Starving Young Bull is a great man. He dances well and long. He goes in for peace strongly. He has given all his blankets and is naked. He has given his one gun and is without arms himself." And the crowd sent up a chorus of applause which my friend drank in and was pleased — as many another man has been when the crowd cheered.

The Blackfeet also in turn danced, and gave presents of what they had, and thus the peace dance went on. Long before it ended, however, I had slipped away to our camp and retired to rest, for we had travelled some distance that day and expected to travel farther on the morrow. We had heard of buffalo coming in from the southeast. The Indians were waiting for them to pass on to the north, when they hoped to build pounds and slaughter them wholesale. We promised to go around the head of the approaching herds and not interfere with the projected plan. This would give us a longer trip, but it was the right thing to do.

Two days later we had killed enough buffalo to load and furnish provisions for men and dogs. We moved camp into a bluff of timber about the centre of our "kill," and while Joseph and Jim made camp and chopped and carried wood, Tommy and I hauled in the meat, which kept us busy until near midnight. Then we had to stage it up and freeze it into shape for our narrow dog sleds. Joseph worked like a good fellow at packing in logs to our woodpile until the stars told him it was midnight and Sunday morning had begun.

We made up our fire and slept through the wintry night. When daylight came we renewed our campfire, cooked our food, thawed some meat, and cut it up into morsels to feed our dogs.

With old Joseph leading, we joined in prayer and sang some hymns. Alternately toasting or freezing as we stood before that huge blaze, we passed the morning hours stoking and stirring and poking. About noon the wind again blew up into a storm, and soon clouds of snow were swirling in every direction.

We were just sitting down to our dinner when, with a weird chanting song there came in out of the storm into the shelter of the camp a tall, wild-looking Blackfoot. We knew that he was not alone. We knew that even then each one of us was covered by the gun or shod-arrow of his companions. Right across from us this strange Indian, without looking at us, sang on.

I looked at my companions. Tommy was pale; Jim was white. Like myself, each was grasping his gun with one hand. I could feel my heartbeats, and it seemed as if my hair was lifting under my cap. Joseph was coolly eating his dinner. Not a muscle changed. Not the faintest appearance of a change of blood showed in his face. Like the stolid philosopher he was, he continued his meal.

The Blackfoot, having finished his song, made a short speech. All this time not a word was uttered on our side. Except for the sound of Joseph crunching his meat, we sat in silence. For three of our party it was truly a solemn time. Then our visitor, having finished his harangue, disappeared as he came. To Joseph, who understood the language, I said, "What did he say?"

Old Joseph swallowed a mouthful of meat, cleared his throat, and replied, "He says there are many of them; their hearts are for peace, and they will come into our camp."

Presently they did come, some forty in all. Ten to one they stood around us. I told them, through Joseph, about their friends we had met in Maskepetoon's camp, and how they had been treated; that the people in the north were all for peace; that it was our work to teach all men that peace and brotherhood was the right thing; that if they wished to camp beside us, we would share our meat with them; that the reason we were not travelling was that this was the "God-day," and we did not travel or hunt on that day; that the Indians who were with me were the near friends of Mon-e-guh-ba-now, and that Mon-e-guh-ba-now was my personal friend.

Then the leader spoke up and said, "We also are for peace. We will camp beside you for tonight. We will not eat your meat. My young men will kill for us. We are glad to hear what you have to say about peace." Then he spoke to his following, and one went out into the storm, and the others went to work clearing away the snow and carrying in wood, and presently they had a big camp arranged within a few feet of ours. Soon their hunter came in, and six or seven followed him out. In an incredibly short time back they came loaded, and the whole crowd was in a little while busy roasting and eating the rich buffalo meat.

I could not help but wonder why these men acted as they now did. A few months since, and they would have killed us. A few months hence, and they would do the same. Now the hard winter, the northerly trend of the buffalo, Maskepetoon's brave act—all this might, and certainly did, influence them. But so many do not think that far ahead of or around their immediate existence.

Are these men moodish? Is this a peace mood? Are human passions subject to cycles? Is this the dip or the arch in the cycle influencing these men, even against themselves, to seek peace? How easily they could have killed us just now; forty to four, and fully half of these bigger than any of us. Do they want our guns and clothes, our blankets and ammunition? For less than this they have planned and killed many times before. What prevents them now? Is the hand of the Lord upon them? Has He work for us to do? Are we immortal till that work is done?

I watched those men. I tried to look beyond the paint and the feathers and the manner of their actions. I mentally photographed them, in groups and individually, and thus the long hours dragged on; for the Sabbath evening had lost its rest for us. Then one of them, who had stuck close to our camp for hours, suddenly revealed that he could speak Cree well. I was glad then that none of us had said anything that might in any way reflect on these men. Undoubtedly he had watched for this. After he had spoken I questioned him and answered his questioning until late at night.

When the Blackfeet began to stretch out around the campfire, we did the same. But with the exception of Joseph, who snored, none of our company slept. At midnight we were astir and harnessing our dogs. We took the meat down from our staging and loaded our sleds, all the time watching our strange companions. The Blackfeet stirred as soon as we did, and about two hours and a half after midnight we each took our own course. Ours was straight for yonder northern mission. Whither our friends went I knew not.

Our arrival home was hailed with satisfaction, for we brought with us meat, and this told of buffalo being within reach. Father and Mother were delighted to hear about Maskepetoon and how he had made peace, for the present at least. Peter had kept at the saw, and the lumber pile was growing. Larsen was busy all the time making necessary furniture and preparing material for the church which we hoped to build in the coming spring.

Our community at this time was made up of the mission party, the Hudson's Bay Company's postmaster and some employees, Mr. Connor and his son Jim.

Christmas found us all well. Our service and the dinner and the games and drives which followed were full of pleasant excitement. We had no organ or choir, but we all sang. We had buffalo boss and tongue, and beaver tail, and moose nose, and wild cat, and prairie chicken, and rabbits, and backfats, and pemmican. We had fast and strong dog teams, and we improvised carioles and had some wild driving over hill and dale. We ran foot races and snowshoe and dog-train races. We played football and made this part of the Saskatchewan valley ring with our shouting and fun. Mr. Steinhauer came over and joined us on New Year's Day and entered into the sports with all the ardour of youth. We all thoroughly enjoyed ourselves.

EIGHTEEN

To the Tents of the Blackfeet

The year 1865 had barely started on its way when there came a courier from Maskepetoon to Father, requesting him if possible to come out and go with him to the Blackfoot camp. The old chief desired to ratify the peace treaty and to lengthen its days as much as possible. Father at once sent him word to make ready, and that he would be out in a few days. He decided to take Peter and me with him. Starting early, travelling fast, and keeping at it late, we reached Maskepetoon's camp the second evening.

Next morning we were away with the chief and some forty of his warriors and head men. The weather was very cold. Father was the only one in the party with a cariole, and this he shared with Maskepetoon. The rest of us were on foot, and as the snow was deep except where the buffalo had trampled it down, our progress was slow.

Other Indians, from camps situated at different points along the eastern and southern fringe of the Beaver Hills, joined us. Among these was a Blackfoot who was taking back a Cree wife. I took occasion to say to her, "Are you not afraid this peace may not last very long?" She merely laughed at my suggestion, but later on it came to pass that this same woman fell a victim to the

Blackfoot she had taken as her husband. It is related of them that a few months after this, while he and some others were gambling on a hill as the camp was moving past, the Cree woman came opposite the gamblers. Her husband said to his companions, "See how I can shoot." Aiming at the woman, he shot her dead in her tracks. An unfeeling laugh from the crowd followed the shocking tragedy.

The third day from Maskepetoon's lodges, we camped within a few miles of the Blackfeet. Early next morning our scouts were every little while bringing us news of the numbers and situation of the camp.

Hardy fellows those scouts were. We were moving at a brisk, quiet walk, but they must run on for miles, and then double on their tracks back to us. While away they must be invisible. They must see all that is to be seen, but remain unseen themselves. To do this they must take the contour of the country, note the condition of the sun and wind, be on the lookout for buffalo, coyotes, wolves, dogs, and ravens, crows, and other fowl. They must keep a constant lookout for contra-scouting, and for this the nose and ear and eye and mind must be always alert. To do this well requires the quickening of every sense. To do all this and to make ten miles an hour on foot requires a depth of lung and strength of limb and purpose of will which heredity and constant practice alone can give.

Our scouts that morning were like telegraph bulletins. We knew how the camp was arranged, and changed our course to suit this arrangement. We were told of the windings of the coulee, or valley, down which the Blackfeet lodges were standing. We were told of hunting parties that had gone out that morning; of the bands of horses and how closely these were guarded; of the long strings of women and ponies, and dogs and travois, which were coming and going in various directions, packing wood to camp.

When close we stopped behind a bluff, while our men put on their visiting paint and dress material. In a few minutes, with their small circular mirrors and ochre bags, our company was transfigured in appearance and colour. Bright colours in garments and on faces made a wonderful change, and to my eye this was exceedingly fitting. The scene was in accord with itself; it was natural.

Everything in the picture was complete and natural and true: the sweep of the valley of the Battle River which slopes from our feet; the ranges of forest-dotted hills, climbing one above the other, from the river's brink even to the limit of our vision; the intersecting fields of snow-clad prairie, reflecting each in its turn the brilliant sunlight; the buffalo that here and there seem like ink dots on the vast ground of dazzling white that stretches far and wide; and the great solitude of primeval nature that broods over all. Then the curling heavenward of the smoke of our temporary fire, the athletic and well-proportioned physique of the men, their costumes and paint. All this was just as it should be, belonging to the place and time.

Now the last feather was tied on, the last touch of vermilion in its place, and we moved on for another hour's quick tramp. A hushed excitement was apparent. This whole thing was yet a very uncertain quantity. The most thoughtless in our party was somewhat checked by the anxiety of the moment.

When the last scout came in we were within a few hundred yards of the camp. Maskepetoon and Father stepped to the front side by side, as the chief would have it. Next came the standard bearers, and the Union Jack and the Hudson's Bay Company's flag were unfurled to the breeze; then the head men and chief warriors; then the young men and scouts. Peter and I brought up the rear with our dog trains.

The horse guards and wood carriers and the children at play were in full view of our advancing column. At first there was a rushing of stock homewards, and a scrambling for the road by those engaged in hauling wood. The children screamed and fled over the hill into the deep, narrow valley in which the lodges were situated. An inexperienced person would never have thought that hundreds of tents, filled with warriors and women and children, were only a short distance from us.

Presently up out of the valley came a swarm of men and boys, all armed and anxious. Then when the older ones recognized Maskepetoon, they began to shout, "Mon-e-guh-ba-now!" and came to meet us gladly. As they came, they fired their guns into the air. Our men did likewise and sang as they marched. In a few minutes we were on the brow of the hill and the Blackfoot camp lay at our feet.

Maskepetoon and Father, with Peter and myself, were taken to the head chief's tent, and hospitably entertained in the style and manner peculiar to this people. Buffalo meat and dried berries constituted the food. The former was served either fresh or dry, or as pounded meat and grease, or as pemmican. The berries were either boiled or eaten dry. The vessels the food was served in were wooden and the ladles it was dipped with were made of horn. Neither of these, so far as I could see, were ever washed. The cooks would cut up the meat for the guests as is done for small children among the white people. While in the Blackfoot camp we had no use for a knife, though we would have infinitely preferred to cut and carve our own food. Father would quietly say, "Look the other way, John." And I would as quietly think, "If he can stand it, how much more can I."

Three Bulls, the chief in whose tent we were, was a tall, dignified old man. His war and hunting days were over, but there was a prestige in his manner and presence which spoke of a history for this man. It was this, no doubt, which kept him in the commanding position he occupied. He had three wives living with him in his tent. These might be described as old, older, oldest. There were two handsome young men, his sons, evidently the children of different mothers. Both father and mothers were very proud of these superb specimens of physical manhood. The work of the camp was done by the chief's daughters-in-law and granddaughters, who came and went without noise or fuss in the discharge of their duties. The trio of wives sat and sewed moccasins or played the role of hostesses.

These were thoroughly buffalo Indians. Without buffalo they would be helpless, and yet the whole nation did not own one. To look at them, and to hear them, one would feel as if they were the most independent of all men; yet the fact was they were the most dependent among men. Moccasins, mittens, leggings, shirts, and robes—all buffalo. With the sinews of the buffalo they stitched and sewed. Their lariats, bridle lines, stirrup-straps, girths, and saddles were manufactured out of buffalo hide. Their women made scrapers out of the leg bone for fleshing hides. The men fashioned knife handles out of the bones, and the children made toboggans of the same. The horns served for spoons and powder flasks.

During our stay in the camp the women and children were frequently sent out of the chief's tent, and then the lodge would be packed with minor chiefs and headmen and warriors who would listen to Maskepetoon and Father. Lively discussions there took place on the benefits of peace among men. Father's descriptions of eastern civilization and Christianity were as strange revelations to these men. They listened and wondered if these things could be true, so different were their experiences of white men from what Father had to tell them of the conduct of our government and of Christian men to the Indians in general. He told them of the many villages and tribes of Indians who were living in harmony and peace right in the midst of the white people. One could see that most of these men were glad of the present respite, and yet there were some who chafed under the necessity of even a short intermission from their business of horse-stealing and scalp-taking.

There was one young war chief in camp who kept aloof from us. As he had considerable influence and a large following, some anxiety was felt by our party and the Blackfeet friendly to us. However, during the second evening of our stay, he came to the chief's tent, and it was announced that he was waiting outside. Our host gathered his robe around him and went out. Presently the proud young chieftain stepped in and took a seat beside us. Later on the old chief returned, and I enquired of Maskepetoon, "Why this unusual ceremony?" He told me that this young warrior chief was the son-in-law of the old man, and it was a rule of etiquette that the son-in-law should not come into a tent while his father-in-law was in it.

This war chief said that he was not very anxious for peace, that war to him was like eating good fruit—he loved it. But, as the others were favourable, he would join them for a while. Then turning to Father, he said, "You must, if you are in earnest, let your son come to my tent and live with me while in our camp." Father asked me if I was willing, and I said, "Yes." So it was arranged that I should go. Presently the young chief signed to me to follow him and we started for his tent.

It was dark as we wended our way in and out among the lodges in the windings of the valley. It seemed to me that the dogs were without number; but a quiet, sharp word from my leader made them shrink away from us, and on we went for quite a distance. Presently we came to a large lodge. The chief motioned me to a reclining couch of buffalo skins, and then began to speak to his wives and to a number of young men who seemed to be his dependents and who were very obedient to his word. In the matter of wives he was four ahead of his father-in-law, having seven to own him lord, the last and youngest being the old chief's daughter.

My host was a tall, athletic fellow, about thirty-five years of age. He had a wild, wicked look about him, was quick and nervous in movement, and was, from appearance at any rate, a man not to be trifled with. I should judge that his wives' ages ranged all the way from eighteen to thirty years, and there were several children. It was the largest lodge I had ever been in and needed two fires to keep us warm. Some of the women untied a bundle of newly dressed robes and made up a couch for me next to the chief's. They handed me some dried meat and berries. After this late supper I turned in for the night.

Before daylight the camp was astir and huge fires were burning in the centre of the lodge. Yet the keen cold was felt just a few feet from them, for our northern January weather was in full sway. As soon as I sat up in my couch, one of the women brought me water in a wooden bowl for my morning ablutions, and I had my pocket-handkerchief to serve as a towel. Then they gave me boiled meat cut into small pieces for breakfast. I longed for salt.

All day strangers kept coming and going in our tent. It seemed to me that I was on exhibition. Once during the day my host signed to me to follow him. We went out to the summit of a hill where his band of horses was driven up by some young men who had them in charge, and I admired the number and quality of his stock. There must have been a hundred or more in the bunch, most of them no doubt the result of his stealings. Then we went back to the tent, and the day passed quietly away.

In the evening a crowd of men occupied the space in the lodge, and much smoking and speech-making went on. I did not understand what they said. Everyone carried his weapons—bow and arrows, flint-lock gun, or war-club. I could readily see that the idea of placing confidence in anyone had not as yet entered the minds of these men. Sometimes they became greatly excited, and as they frequently nodded or pointed to me, I could not help but imagine all manner of trouble. Finally the crowd dispersed, and I was still alive. When all was quiet I settled down into a sound sleep.

Long before daylight the big fires were blazing and crackling, faintly forcing back the fearful cold which had taken possession of the thin-walled and unfloored lodge during the few hours in which the camp slept. I was up with the dawn trying to thaw myself out, but did not fully succeed until I had breakfasted.

In the evening a number of Blood Indians arrived, and a dance was organized in our tent. Proud arrogance and intense self-sufficiency seemed to speak out in their every word and action. One would think they were the aristocracy of the plains. The meeting was more than a dance; it was an experience meeting. Each one recited his deeds of daring and acted in pantomime the approach, the ambush, the charge, and the shooting, stabbing, scalping, and horse-taking of his past. With frantic energy these men told of their various deeds of valour, and every now and then a comrade, a living witness, would shout, "It is true! I was there!" At this the crowd applauded, and the drums beat, while the next man sprang to his feet, and leaped, danced, whooped and sang. Then when the drums ceased, he too would vaunt his feats of valour.

All this was at first quite interesting to me; but as the hours went by and it grew past midnight, I wished the ball would break up. Since there seemed no immediate prospect of this happening, I stepped out into the night. I wended my way up the valley until I came to the old chief's tent. There I raked the coals together and made up a fire, as the night was bitterly cold. I saw that Father and Peter were asleep. Maskepetoon was stretched in his blanket between Father and the fire. I got down in front of Maskepetoon and gradually crept under his blanket until he gave it to me. He got up, made more fire, and sat and smoked for the rest of the night while I slept with a profound sense of rest and security beside my friends once more. Many a time in after days Maskepetoon would joke with me about taking his blanket from him when in the Blackfoot camp.

The next day we started for home. We might have peace for three months or less. This was the impression on our minds. The people on both sides were too widely scattered and too independent of each other, and the range of country too big, to hope for any permanent peace. Still, even a short respite was something to be grateful for. Our route home was more direct and we travelled much faster than in coming. The buffalo had been moving north and in their progress had trampled the snow for miles in many places. We found that Muddy Bull had several animals staged ready for us, so Father piled the camp equipment and our provisions into his cariole, and Peter and I took the loads of meat.

We reached the mission on the second evening from Maskepetoon's camp. All were well and wonderfully pleased to see us back. Peter resumed his work of lumber-making, and I that of bringing in provisions.

NINETEEN

Buffalo Pound

My provision-hauling crew for the next two months was made up of my old friend Joseph and a young Indian named Susa.

We started at once back to the Cree camp with four trains of dogs. Near noon the next day we came to vast herds of buffalo, and one of my trains ran away with the buffalo. For a time we could see them, but soon they went out of sight in the distance. Leaving the other train to my men, I set out in pursuit of the runaways. For miles I was able to track them; then the buffalo became so numerous ahead of me that all trace of the dogs was lost. As the course they ran nearly paralleled our road out, I kept on until late, and after running some twenty miles had to give them up and strike out to head off my men.

We reached the Cree camp that night. The Indians sympathized with me in my loss and promised to keep on the lookout for the dogs. I felt the loss keenly, for they were young dogs, were developing handsomely, and shaping to become "flyers."

The camp we were now in was called in Cree "sitting by the place of bringing them in." This would mean in English, "pound-keeping." The situation of a pound was generally on the south or east side of a gently rising hill, the west or north side of this hill being prairie or open country and the east or south side of it timber. In this timber, not far from the summit, the Cree pound was erected.

The pound was made by chopping and clearing away the timber from a circular space, say, one hundred or one hundred and twenty-five feet in diameter. From this circle all the brush and trees, with the exception of one tree in the centre, were cleared out. Around this circle a strong fence of logs and brush was built, strong enough and high enough to hold the buffalo. At the entrance, which was made about twenty feet wide, a causeway or sloping corduroy bridge was built up of timber so that there was a "jump off" into the pound of about three feet.

From the entrance on either side a strong brush and log fence was run out towards the north or west as was convenient. These lines of fence gradually diverged as they left the corral until, at the end of a hundred yards or more, they were almost that distance apart. From the ends of the fence bundles of willows were placed on end at regular intervals for a mile or more. These were called "watching waiters." Their outside terminals were fully a mile apart.

While the pound, the fence, and the "waiters" were being built, the conjurers of the camp were making "strong medicine" to give luck and magnetism to the pound. For days and nights these medicine-makers and general dealers in the supernatural had pounded their drums and sung themselves hoarse. Now that the pound was ready for dedication, they organized a procession and went on with the consecration of the pound. With solemn visage and in dignity of attitude, these priests of the old faith took their places at the head of the procession. With their medicine-bags in hand they stood like statues, while the rest formed in line, drummers and singers next to the priests.

Then the whole camp, or as many as could attend, followed. At a signal the drums beat, the song was raised at the head, and then taken up all along the whole line. To time they stepped away around the bluff, and turning into the fence came down the lane, up over the causeway, and jumped into the pound. Turning to the left, they marched around the circle of the pound. Then with short petitionary speeches, the conjurers proceeded to hang their medicine-bags on the limbs of the lone tree which stood in the centre. This done, the pound was dedicated, consecrated, and declared ready for use.

The next thing needed was buffalo. The man who had fat horses, and who desired the tongues of the buffalo, many or few that might be brought into the pound in one "fetch", would take his horse, saddled and bridled, to the tent of an expert at "bringing in." He would say, "Here is my horse; now go after them." Then the O-noh-che-buh-how, or "Who-Goes-After-Them," makes ready. Slowly, with dignity, as one upon whom a grave responsibility is thrust but perfectly conscious of being the only man to bear it, he mounts the horse and rides forth.

He is keenly watched by the lookouts on high ground. The whole camp is in a flutter of excitement. Is the time right? Are the spirits friendly? Will the medicine work? Will "Who-Brings-Them-In" be wise in his handling of the buffalo? Is the pound properly located? Everybody is anxious about the new, untried pound.

Now those on the lookout are making signs and throughout the camp is shouted, "He has started a herd!" Another sign. "The herd is a big one!" That electrifies every man, woman and child in the encampment.

Behold, there is another sign and the joyful news rings forth: "They are coming straight!" Then the signal is given, "Make ready, to your places." There is a movement by all the able-bodied men to the lines of fence which reach out from the door of the pound. There they place themselves opposite to one another. Behind the fence, and even beyond it, behind heaps of snow and brush the men lie in waiting until the head of the herd passes them, when from each side they rise simultaneously and urge the buffalo on into the pound.

While all this is going on near the pound and in the camp, "Mr. Who-Brings-Them-In" is doing his level best with brain and voice and horse. Lay of country and direction of wind are noted. As he rode out he looked at the position of the sun. He pulled a little of the hair off his robe and let it go above his head to determine the exact direction of the wind. This he did on a hill so that the movement of air would not be influenced by hills and valleys.

When he sighted the buffalo, he stopped. Lighting his pipe, he thought out the whole plan as well as he could, with the known quantities before him. For what was as yet unknown, he held his pipe-stem skyward and humbly petitioned the spirits to help him. Then he shook his pipe, detached the stem, and put both into his fire-bag.

Remounting his horse, he started for the buffalo. If these were scattered he set out to bunch them. Riding slightly to windward and dismounting, he pulled a small bunch of dried grass out of his bosom, and chipping off a bit of punk he placed it on his flint. He struck this with his steel. When the punk caught fire, he dropped it into a little nest he had prepared in the grass. Then he waved this to and fro, and if the grass caught fire soon he was satisfied. If not, he took a few grains of powder from his horn and dropped them on the spark of fire on the punk, making a flame which speedily ignited the grass. In a very little time the keen-scenting buffalo would notice the tiny puff of smoke and move together.

Having bunched the buffalo, if they moved in the right direction he let them go and quietly watched them from a distance. If they went to one side, he headed them back either with a whiff of smoke as before or by letting them catch a glimpse of himself. Thus he brings them within the long line of "watching waiters." Now the herd is becoming excited and begins to move rapidly. Riding close, he heads them on. If they rush too fast one way, he drops behind and rides across their track the other way. At a quick gallop, he utters a series of strange cries which seem to be almost hypnotic in their influence, for the head of the bunch moves as if in response to the weird cry.

When the herd is going as he wants, he talks to them encouragingly. "That is right, O mother cow; you are doing well. Keep right on. You will gladden many hearts, you will fill many stomachs, you will warm and cover many bodies." Then he would give his shrill cry. I have ridden beside these men when bringing in buffalo and it has seemed to me as if they had bridles in the mouths of the leaders of the herds who jumped to do their bidding. The man seemed transformed, energized, intensely consecrated, and thus his spirit became masterful and strong in its purpose.

Now the lines of "watching waiters" are rapidly converging. The side-to-side rushes of the excited herd are becoming shorter and follow one another in quick succession. Both man and buffalo are approaching the crucial point. It is now but two or three hundred yards to the end of the lines of brush. If the herd should break to either side before these are reached, the driver will be humiliated, the new pound made unlucky, and the whole camp sadly disappointed.

"Who-Brings-Them-In" feels all this and makes supreme effort; he throws his whole soul into the work. He calls, he urges, he petitions, he rides fearlessly and recklessly. Now the head of the herd is past the first of the line of concealed men. These rise together, and others, and others, and on in a mad, wild rush sweep the deceived and thoroughly affrighted buffalo over the "jump-off" and into the pound. "Who-Brings-Them-In" stays not for congratulations, but gallops to his tent, leaps from the horse, rushes in to his couch, and flings himself on it, exhausted but triumphant. Perhaps that afternoon, to help him fully recover, some old friend will give him a Turkish bath.

What surprised me was that these men who went after buffalo and endured such physical hardship and nervous strain did not receive any more than the rest in the sharing of the buffalo. The man who owned the horse got the tongues. Those men who did the wonderful work of bringing in had the glory. Like the chiefs who planned and lived for the people, without any remuneration, they were the patriots of the camp.

I have described what happened when the buffalo were convenient to camp, say, two or three hours distant. Often they were much farther away. Then the process was different. Another expert would start from camp on foot and travel twenty, thirty, or fifty miles into the north or west country. At last, finding a suitable herd, he would slowly work them by stratagem and by smoke and by scent towards the pound. Sometimes he would have to wait for hours for a "convenient season." Sometimes he would of necessity run for miles as fast as his strength and wind would permit, in order to turn the trend of movement into a more favourable direction. Thus, after wearying days and nights, his bunch of buffalo would be sighted from the lookout. Then "Who-Brings-Them-In" would ride forth and meet him, take the herd in his turn, and the foot man would return to camp and rest.

When the last buffalo was over the "jump off," he was not far behind the rest, for the crowd of yelling Indians were at the heels of the herd. When all were in, the door or gap was suddenly filled by a solid line of men. They pulled their robes before them and stood without a move as the mad herd settled into a gallop around the pound, always running as the medicine man had walked — with the sun. In the meantime the pound was surrounded by the people of the camp, all rejoicing because of the success of the enterprise. Pound and medicine and men had all been blessed, and the hearts of the people were thankful.

The twang of an arrow told that the work of slaughter had begun. This was continued with arrow and flint-lock until all the large animals in the herd were dead. Then the boys were turned into the pound to fight the calves. Many a chase the calves gave them, sometimes driving the boys back up on the timber and brush of the walls of the pound. When all were dead, someone deputed for the duty would mount the back of a dead bull or big cow and apportion the hunt.

"Hollow-Back, you take that one. Crooked Legs, there is yours. Bear's Child, this is for you. Wolf Teeth, cut that one up."

And so, in stentorian voice, this man would divide the spoil. Soon the pound was full of men and women taking off the robes, cutting up the meat, and packing these to the tents. In a little while the new pound was left to the dogs, who in their turn held high carnival among the refuse, fighting and feeding to the full.

Not one buffalo was allowed to escape. The young and the poor must die with the strong and fat, for it was believed that if these were spared they would tell the rest, and so make it impossible to bring any more buffalo into a pound.

We were staying in Muddy Bull's lodge. The weather was intensely cold. All through that January the mercury never rose above 10° below zero and it fell to 50° below. In our lodge, which was one of the best, we were passably cosy with our ordinary travelling costumes on and with a blanket robe over our shoulders and a brisk fire in the centre of the tent. Even then we had to turn around every little while and "warm the other side." Great brisk fires were kept in these thin leather homes of our Indian people.

To keep those huge fires going during the cold winter months gave the women and girls of the camps constant employment. They accepted the labour and drudgery cheerfully and could be seen at all hours of the day stringing over the hills and across the plains with dogs and horses and travois, their own backs loaded to the utmost carrying capacity with wood.

The life of an Indian woman in those early days was an extremely busy one. Packing and unpacking dogs and horses, making camps, providing wood, making and mending moccasins and wearing apparel, cooking, cutting, drying, and pounding meat, rendering grease, chopping bones to get out the marrow fat, making pemmican, stretching, scraping and dressing buffalo hides to make robes or leather—a long tedious process, in which not only the brains of the worker were needed in order to excel, but also those of the dead animals—kept her going early and late. Besides all this, the manufacturing of saddles, travois, tents, and shagganappi also devolved upon the women. Yet they seemed to be contented and happy, and with true feminine resource still found time to give to attire and adornment, and the practising of all those mysterious arts which have charmed and magnetized the other sex. No wonder these women and girls were at a premium and cost all the way from a blanket up to a band of stolen horses. The more of them a man had, then the greater man was he.

Nor was the life of the male Indian altogether that of a sinecure. Somehow or other the idea has gone abroad that these Indians led a very lazy life. If the man who has ever thought this had spent some time with either wood or plain Indians and had accompanied them on their hunting and war expeditions, he would change his views.

To follow a wood hunter on foot from before daylight in the short days, through brush and copse and heavy timber, over big hills and across wide valleys, on and on for many miles, sometimes until noon or late in the afternoon before a "kill" is made; or having started game, to run for miles at a terrific pace, hoping to head off the quarry and at last secure a shot; then, having killed, to butcher or secure from wolf, or coyote, or wolverine, the desired meat and strike as straight as possible for the camp, sometimes many many miles distant, with thick forest and dense darkness now intervening; or it may be to have all the labour and exhaustion of such a chase without the chance of a shot, reaching camp late at night wearied and disappointed. To continue this for days, sometimes feasting and again famishing — and all this not from choice but of necessity — could be counted no easy matter. It is not for fun, but life.

It may be with the same wood hunter you start a prime buck moose or elk during those glorious days in the beginning of autumn, and he bounds away in his strength and swiftness. Your Indian says, "We must run him down," and leads off in long, regular strides, and for a time you feel as if your lungs were in your throat and your heart is beating a double tattoo. Over and under fallen timber, down precipitous banks, up steep hills, and it takes some time for you to "catch your second wind," and to brace up your will and say to yourself, "I am also a man," and then settle down like your Indian to steady work.

He, however, is doing more than you, who are but following him. He is noting lay of land and direction of wind, calculating in order to cut across where your game may have gone around, watching the tracks, gauging the distance the buck is ahead of you, noting the settling of the earth at edge of pool or creek where the big fellow left his tracks as he ran, and you are encouraged and spurred on, or contrariwise, as the crafty hunter tells you in hushed tones what he knows.

Then by and by, after an hour or two, or three, perhaps, of such work, you stand beside the fallen carcass and wipe your forehead and wish you had a dozen towels; but while your exultations and congratulations are hot within you, a word of caution comes from the Indian beside you: "The sun is low and the camp is far; let us hurry," and the work of butchering and skinning the meat goes on, till presently, with a load of meat on your back, you start for the distant camp. Not in any sense is this a lazy life.

Or it may be your hunter friend is in for a "fur-hunt," and you start with him to make a line of dead-falls for marten, or to hang a hundred or so snares for lynx. The snow is deep, and at every step several pounds of it fall in on your snowshoe; but from early morn until late in the evening you tramp and toil, chopping and stooping and grunting over snare and dead-fall, and when night is on, having carried your provisions, blanket, and kettle all day, besides the baits for dead-falls and snares for lynx traps, you dig away the deep snow, cut some wood, and make a fire for the night. While the fire burns, you doze and chill, and pile on fuel and wait for morning, only to repeat yesterday's work, and so on, until, having made a big detour and hung your snares and carefully fixed your dead-falls, you in three or four days reach home. Then in a short time you must visit all these, and in the intervening days make your forays for food. No one who has tried this manner of obtaining a living will pronounce it a lazy life.

But suppose you were some plains or buffalo Indians, and, as was about the average condition in the winter-time, the buffalo were from fifty to two hundred miles from your camp—the rigour of the winter and the condition of grass and wood forbidding the camp moving any nearer to them—the hunting parties had constantly to be organized and the meat and robes brought home over long distances. Under such circumstances the hunter not only had to undergo great hardships, but also to run very great risks. There were deep snow and darkness and dangerous storms on the bleak, treeless plains. The really indolent man would not engage in such work.

Then, it was incumbent upon every able-bodied man, under the code of honour of the time, to make an annual or bi-annual or even more frequent foray for horses and scalps. These trips generally took place in the spring and fall. With the melting of snow and ice in spring, or the making of the same in autumn, parties large and small would be made up. Each with lariat and a few pairs of moccasins, and, if possessed of a gun, with as much ammunition as he could obtain, or armed with bow and quiver full of shod arrows, these men would start in the dead of night for the enemy's country, depending on sustaining life by the chase on their way.

Journeying on, sometimes by day and sometimes by night, fording rapid streams and swimming wide rivers, through ice-cold water — these must be considered as trifles. By and by, when the enemy's presence is felt, there will come the weary watching and waiting, amid cold and hunger; for cunning and strategy are now pitted the one against the other, and endurance and pluck must back these up or the trip will be a failure. One, two, three hundreds of miles of steady tramping, with your camp always facing in the direction of where your enemy is supposed to be. Every day or night the scouts, making thrice the distance covered by the party, keep up their constant effort to discover and forestall counter war-parties, or to find the enemy's camp; and when this is found sometimes to hang for days on its movements, and, following up, watch for a favourable spot and time either to make a charge or to steal in under cover of storm or darkness and drive off bands of horses.

Then in either case to start for home, and push on regardless of weather so long as men and horses will hold out. After a successful raid those long runs for home were great tests of horse-flesh and human endurance. With scalded legs, blistered feet and weary limbs, and with eyes heavy for want of sleep, these men, now exultant with victory, would vie with each other in the race for camp.

Furthermore, upon the men and boys of the camp devolved the care of the horses. The herding and guarding of these gave many a weary tramp or ride, and many a night in cold and storm, without sleep or rest. And finally, the constant need of protecting their camps from the wily enemy was a source of permanent worry, and always pressed as a heavy responsibility upon these men.

In such trials of endurance and hardship, there was assuredly no place for a lazy man.

By two o'clock in the morning we are up boiling our kettle and snatching a bite of breakfast. By four o'clock sleds are loaded with five to six hundred pounds of frozen meat and dogs are harnessed and we bid Mr. and Mrs. Muddy Bull a hasty good-bye. We will make the sixty-mile drive home in the day if we can.

At the mission the event of the winter was the arrival of the February packet from Fort Garry. It might only bring a few letters from Eastern friends and two or three newspapers several months old; but this was the one connecting link. The dwellers in the Hudson's Bay posts and at mission stations in the North-West, though far apart, felt a common interest in this packet, which not only brought news from the East but also from one another. For days before its expected arrival at the post or mission, the packet was the chief item of conversation. Many an eye was turned to the direction whence it should come. Many a person the last thing at night would stand out in the cold and listen for the sound of bells which might indicate the approach of the eagerly looked-for mail. And when at last it came, how many were disappointed. The one lone chance, and still no news where so much had been expected.

And for the swarthy-faced, wiry-built, hardy men who brought this packet, as you looked at them you could see fifty miles a day stamped on their every move — fifty miles and more through deep snow, blinding storms and piercing cold. Picked men these were, and they knew it, and held themselves accordingly, heroes for the time being at every post they touched. Nor did these faithful fellows tarry long at any one place. Arriving in the morning, they were away the same afternoon. This was the manner of their faithful service to the great Company which somehow or other had the faculty of inspiring its employees with splendid loyalty.

Coming home another time with provisions, we stopped at the camp of a solitary hunter, John Whitford by name, where we found our missing dog team. John said that he heard a jingle of bells and expected some travellers were either coming to or passing his camp. Then, hearing no further sounds, he went out to see what it was, when he found Maple alone in harness, but dragging the other four sets of harness behind her. Evidently the sled had caught in some bush and the young dogs had become impatient, and one by one wriggled out of their bonds. Then the wise old mother dog had gone back to the sled and bitten off the traces close up to it, thus freeing herself from the sleigh and saving the harness. She then started for home, stopped to rest by the way at John's camp, where we found her with her pups.

So, through storm and cold, and sometimes over very heavy roads or no roads at all, Joseph, Susa, and I kept at the work of providing for our mission party. Those at home in the meantime were constantly busy holding meetings, doctoring the sick, taking out timber, whipsawing lumber, or hauling hay and wood.

TWENTY ⋘

Newlywed

March of 1865 was a stormy month. About the middle of the month we made another trip to Pigeon Lake. Our purpose was to take in some provisions, together with the plough which was being ironed at Edmonton. As old Joseph knew the country well, we hoped to find a straighter road than the one I had taken before.

At Edmonton, the blacksmith began to question me as to what we intended to do at Pigeon Lake. I told him that Father hoped to establish a mission there.

"Well," said he, "you want to delude some more people with your fanciful stories about God and heaven and hell."

"Do you not believe in God?" I asked.

"No, I do not," was the emphatic answer I received.

A strange feeling came over me. The wild storm, the lonely night, the savage beast had never worried me very much. But here was something new and awful to my young and unsophisticated mind. I was afraid of that man. I took the plough and went away as quickly as I could.

The next day, when we were away from the Fort on our journey, I told my companions. Susa's eyes fairly bulged with astonishment. Old Joseph said, "He must be without any mind."

We took the straight course for Pigeon Lake. Old Joseph now became guide. This was the scene of his young manhood. Here he had trapped beaver, tracked and slain moose and elk. Here huge grizzlies had fallen at the crack of his old flint-lock. Long years ago he had helped to make this small, winding trail. With unerring memory and skill the old man picked up the road and on we went slowly through the deep snow and across bits of prairie. All 'round looked the same, but without a miss we would again enter the bush on the unused trail. It must have taken centuries to develop a brain capable of thus having printed upon it the topography of a country.

We found the cache Oliver and I had made, still secure, but surrounded with the tracks of a wolverine. Into this cache we put the balance of the provisions we had brought and placed the plough on top.

We then retraced our steps back to the camp we had left in the morning, reached Edmonton the next night, and were home in a day and a half.

About the end of March we gave up the provision-hauling trips for the season.

Then I got married. My bride was the daughter of the Rev. H. B. Steinhauer. I had met her in the autumn of 1862, when I accompanied Father on his first visit to Whitefish Lake. Our acquaintance, which had grown into a courtship on my part, was now between two and three years old. Our parents willingly gave us their consent and blessing.

Father and Peter accompanied us to Whitefish Lake, and Father married us in the presence of my wife's parents and people. Our "honeymoon trip" was to drive from Whitefish Lake to Victoria by dog train when the season was breaking up.

After a short sojourn at Victoria we set out to establish the new mission at Pigeon Lake. The Board of Missions had not as yet consented to or approved of such a course, but Father was thoroughly impressed with the wisdom and necessity of such action. Finally he told me that I ought to go and begin work out there. "You can live where any man can," he said. Of course I was proud to have Father think this of me. At the time there was not a dollar of appropriation from the Missionary Society. But Father gave us a pair of four-point Hudson's Bay blankets, two hundred ball and powder, and some net twine, together with his confidence and blessing.

To which Mother said, "Amen."

This book was designed by John Zehethofer
Type-set on linofilm by Mono Lino Typesetting Co. Ltd.
Typeface: Palatino
Printed in Canada by The Alger Press Limited